Conflict and Leadership

Conflict and Leadership

How to Harness the Power of Conflict to Create Better Leaders and Build Thriving Teams

Christian Muntean

 BUSINESS EXPERT PRESS

First published in 2018 by
Business Expert Press, LLC
222 East 46th Street, New York, NY 10017
www.businessexpertpress.com

ISBN-13: 978-1-63157-960-8 (paperback)
ISBN-13: 978-1-63157-961-5 (e-book)

Business Expert Press Human Resource Management and Organizational Behavior Collection

Collection ISSN: 1946-5637 (print)
Collection ISSN: 1946-5645 (electronic)

Cover and interior design by Exeter Premedia Services Private Ltd., Chennai, India

First edition: 2018

10 9 8 7 6 5 4 3 2 1

Printed in the United States of America.

I would like to dedicate this book to my wife Marta. You've borne the brunt of it as I've learned and tried to be consistent in applying the principles in this book. Thank you for your patience and grace!

Additionally, I'd like to dedicate this book to the organization and staff of Medair. They are some of the finest and most dedicated humanitarian professionals in the world. I'm grateful for the opportunity to have served with you.

Lastly, I'd like to dedicate this book to Jacob Kuju Lokine. You laid your life down. I miss you.

Abstract

Conflict is one of the greatest sources of tolerated business expenses and loss. This is despite the fact that this expense and loss can, in most cases, be easily turned around to revenue and gain. In the nonprofit world one of the greatest inhibitors of mission success is not that there isn't enough funding, or the challenging nature of the cause. It is the simple fact that teams struggle to work well together.

What if conflict was the starting point for developing trust? What if it catalyzed a deeper, more meaningful understanding between team members? What if it was crucial for building stronger and more powerful organizations? Last of all, what if there were simple steps you could take to automatically help your teams communicate and work together more easily? This book shows you how.

Keywords

conflict resolution at work, how to handle conflict at work, team building, team culture, team leadership, workplace culture

Contents

Foreword

I once consulted with a Fortune 100 company that was wasting huge amounts of time on nonproductive meetings. (Ever hear of that problem before? Perhaps nearby?) I found out within a week that any scheduled meeting was preceded by a half-dozen *unscheduled* meetings intended to deal with any conflicts in advance. Within this crazy paradigm, the company's management thought that it could claim a consensus, collaborative approach.

What it had created was calamitous and chaotic.

It's funny that when you get paid people tend to listen to you, so I convinced them to end the "pre-meeting meetings" cold turkey, and to adopt this phrase when conflict arose during the scheduled meetings: "Let's put the dead rat on the table." (No sense keeping it under the table when everyone knew by the stench that it was there.)

That simple difference saved that company well over a million dollars annually, earned me six figures, and made me a local hero.

We tend to think of "the power of conflict" or "creative conflict" as weasel words—those that are self-denying, such as "thunderous silence" or "militant pacifists." However, those of us who have observed organizations (as I have or over 30 years), public and private, large and small, domestic and foreign, have come to understand that conflict is unavoidable among bright people, and that the energy and passion it ignites can be directed to highly positive ends.

Christian Muntean has successfully parsed the language and emotions of conflict to create a fascinating, highly enjoyable, and most pragmatic approach so that any company can use conflict positively and continually. He discusses the various kinds, distills emotion from important issues, and provides insights into how to be resilient and stronger as a result. The fact that he's done this for years with his clients creates a firm, unchallengeable approach to what too many people believe to be unapproachable.

Warfare is actually the least subtle form of communication. Most sane people would agree that discussion trumps hostility. Conflict is a condition of communication if we choose to make it so. It's a condition of warfare if we choose to make it so.

Conflict and Leadership is about understanding across the table, not battle in the arena. In an age of polarization, agendas, and media-fed opinions, that's something we can all use.

—Alan Weiss, PhD
—Author, *Million Dollar Consulting, Million Dollar Maverick, and over 60 other books*

Acknowledgments

Many people have been involved with helping me shape and ultimately write the concepts in this book. I'd like to acknowledge Alan Weiss for challenging me to write, helping me to outline the content, and for threatening to write a book on this topic if someone else didn't. I'd also like to acknowledge the encouragement of Pat Parnell, Richard Irwin, Rodney Sawyer, and Katherine Gottlieb, all of whom played key roles in nudging me to step out and serve others through peacebuilding. I'd like to recognize David Schlachter who mentored and encouraged me as a green mediator. Finally, I'm thankful for Jesus Christ who teaches me to walk the way of grace and peace.

Introduction

Smooth seas never make skillful sailors.

—Unknown

It may seem like this is a book about conflict or conflict resolution. It isn't. Not at the core. This is a book about becoming a more competent and confident leader. A leader who can face the inevitable storm with skill and grace.

It's in those storms that the most skillful leaders are needed. It is also these storms that provide the greatest opportunities to grow your leadership skills. People don't need great leadership when the way is clear and easy. They need it when the storm threatens. This book may not make your seas become any smoother. But they no longer need to be so dark and intimidating.

What defines leadership skill or success is a widely debated topic. Leadership success may look different if you are a military commander, a business executive, a church leader, or the director of an arts cooperative. However, there are commonalities. This book identifies successful leaders as those who bring the best out of people. They are the men and women who do the most to improve the opportunity and condition of others. I define these people as successful leaders because they are the people that others most naturally want to follow. They don't need to coerce or bribe others. They truly lead. They don't need to drive or herd or manipulate. They are given trust. So, people follow.

All leadership and followership is a relationship. Leadership only exists within the context of this relationship. This is why the best leaders have mastered the art of relating well. That's what this book is about: helping you master your ability to relate well when it is difficult; when you feel challenged, threatened, hurt, abandoned, betrayed, or whatever it might be. Those are some of the most serious leadership storms. Then, having learned this, to create a team and organization which can do the same.

I don't come naturally to conflict resolution. For that matter, I don't come naturally to relating to others with grace. The reason I value both so much is because I have such an intimate knowledge of the alternative.

As I was writing this introduction at a coffee shop, I was interrupted by two leaders who were past clients. Just a few years ago, they were enmeshed in a deep, emotional conflict. They are now able to enjoy each other's trust and company. They can joke about the past, which at the time seemed like the cliff at the end of the world. They attribute much of the recent rapid and strong growth of their organization to the lessons they learned in that conflict.

My hope for you is this book will be a compass and map to help you grow as a leader and to build a robust team who can successfully navigate any relational storm you might encounter.

Christian Muntean, Anchorage, Alaska January 29, 2018

CHAPTER 1

The Nature of Conflict: What it Means, Where it Originates, Why it Gets So Weird

My Messy Story

In 2003, I was hired to advise on peace building in Southern[1] Sudan. At that time, Southern Sudan was at the tail end of decades of civil war, drought, and famine. Secretary of State Colin Powell was driving peace talks forward. However, as anyone who's spent time in conflict zones knows, building peace isn't peaceful. It's unstable territory. It shifts balances of power. It changes the economy. It creates unknown, unfamiliar dynamics that are difficult and sometimes dangerous to navigate.

I was hired by the disaster relief agency, Medair—the primary medical provider in the eastern half of Southern Sudan. Their questions were: How will our work be impacted by peace? Can our programs contribute toward building peace? And, if so, how?

In Kenya, I joined the rest of the research team: Alfred, a Kenyan sociologist, and our team leader; Rebekka, a German psychologist; and Jacob, a Sudanese cultural liaison and interpreter. Within 2 weeks of my arrival, as we prepared to begin field research, I became locked into an intractable conflict with Alfred.

---

[1] In 2003, the region currently known as the country of South Sudan was the southern half of the country of Sudan. It was commonly referred to as Southern Sudan.

Communication shut down. Attempts to talk and to resolve the situation were ineffective. I felt frustrated and angry. Unable to work together, Alfred and I split efforts. We conducted two separate research projects. We produced two separate papers. We offered two separate presentations and conclusions to Medair. About peace.

Medair sent us, separately, to counseling. The counselors didn't know what to do. So, we did what most professionals do. We stewed. We avoided each other. We waited until our contracts ended.

The irony of this experience ate at me. I felt embarrassed professionally. Here I was, studying and advising on peace building, yet, unable to get along with my colleague. I felt helpless. I felt like I had failed an opportunity to serve both the agency and a world region that deserved better.

I also realized that conflict was a constant presence in my life. As much as I preferred to blame other people for it, I had to acknowledge the one constant variable was me.

This experience drove me to learn about how I could relate to conflict differently. I accepted that conflict was inevitable. If I couldn't avoid it, I knew I had to learn how to engage with it more effectively.

This was a challenging, slow, and messy process. It was full of false starts. But I learned. I grew. I changed. I am still growing.

Here is the hope: Learning to engage conflict well is very possible. It is also a powerful key to personal transformation and professional growth. It's well worth it.

For the first few years, I didn't even consider trying to add peace building or dispute resolution to the list of professional services I offered. I focused, instead, on trying to change me. As I changed, others seemed to notice. This resulted in others beginning to ask for help with their conflicts and difficult conversations. That grew into part of my professional tool belt.

Now, helping people navigate disputes and build stronger relationships and healthier organizations has become an area of expertise.

Before we examine how to relate well to conflict, let's answer an important question: What is conflict?

Conflict's Usual Definition and Why it Doesn't Help Anyone

According to the Oxford English Dictionary, conflict is defined as ("Conflict | Definition of Conflict in English by Oxford Dictionaries" 2017):

- A serious disagreement or argument, typically a protracted one
- A prolonged armed struggle
- An incompatibility between two or more opinions, principles, or interests

When the definitions above are our only ways of understanding what we experience as conflict, our options are usually very limited: We can try to escape conflict, attempt to avoid it, or decide we must win it.

This is exactly what the person or people on the other side of our conflict are simultaneously attempting to do. So, the conflict protracts. We arm ourselves, sometimes figuratively, sometimes literally. The sides remain incompatible. The definition above is only helpful in identifying conflict. It doesn't help address it, at all.

Here is a slightly improved definition: *Conflict exists any time there is a disagreement over something important to all sides.*

The change in this definition is nuanced. But it's a critical nuance. The difference is the words: *something important.* Typically, I know the conflict I'm involved in is about something important to *me.* But usually, I think about the other side as being stubborn, arrogant, unjust, and irrational.

However, what if I accepted (even if it didn't make any sense to me) there was something important to the person I'm in conflict with? What if they weren't simply being a jerk or being irrational? What if they were afraid there was something they might not gain or something they could lose in this situation? What if I could discover that?

Would that, possibly, change the conversation?

The answer is, "Yes," it does. It changes the conversation dramatically. Having mediated hundreds of disputes, I've discovered, about 90 percent of the time, people find agreement. I've seen this between executives and boards, teams and departments, majority and minority leaders in the legislature, environmental groups and industry, and parents trying to understand and navigate co-parenting.

What does this tell us? People don't really want to be stuck in a fight. We really don't. Instead, we desire a way through it. We just don't know how to achieve resolution. And we're afraid that resolution might cost us.

At a deep level, people want resolution. Which brings me to my favorite definition of conflict.

A Better Definition of Conflict and Why It Makes All the Difference

Conflict = Opportunity!

People don't fight over things they don't care about. Underneath the nonsense of many arguments, there is something that's deeply important to those involved. Often the surface argument, or position, has become symbolic for something deeper.

I once mediated a dispute between a nonprofit executive director and the associate director. The executive director "Jim" had founded the nonprofit and had steadily grown it over many years. It had regionwide presence and impact. He had met "Sarah" and realized that she could bring tremendous value to the organization. So, he created the associate director role and hired her. Unfortunately, shortly after Sarah was hired she began to insist that she be given Jim's position. She framed this from the perspective of social justice and gender equality.

Jim attempted to placate her by creating a coexecutive director position. This created role confusion between the two. The board rightfully intervened and affirmed a single executive director role. She was unwilling to accept and I was called.

I'm simplifying the story quite a bit, but the surface position for Sarah, in this case, was the position of "Social justice will be achieved with a woman executive (herself) in this organization." We carefully explored this. There was no one else in the organization or in the population they served who felt that the organization was preserving an unjust status quo of male leadership. It began to appear that, for her, the cause of gender equality and gaining the executive director role was symbolic of a much deeper need. That is her legitimate need to feel valued and validated.

Unfortunately, no role can fill that need for someone else. As a result of the board's affirmation of a single executive director, she resigned. She moved on and has continued a career trend of not being able to maintain any position for more than two or three years.

To my knowledge, she's been highly valued everywhere she has gone. I suspect she carries inside of herself a sense that she is "not enough." So, she begins to demand a recognition that is often already given. This creates friction and conflict and eventually she moves on again.

Like Sarah in the story, it is very common that we aren't even aware of what that deeper *something* is. Not only are we often unaware of what is truly important to us, but we are also completely oblivious to what might be important to other side. In the story above, Sarah diminished Jim's years of commitment and personal sacrifice to build a nonprofit that impacted many lives. She was unable to recognize that a position had been created for her precisely *because* she was viewed as valuable. Our needs and how we view symbols can obscure our perspective of reality.

Some of us might even feel like it's a compromise to even explore or listen to another person's perspective. When I was younger, I was convinced that giving a competitive perspective "airtime" would just validate their opinion. Instead, in interpersonal communication, refusing to allow someone to express themselves more often inflames the conflict and causes them to entrench in their position.

In the workplace, disputes over differing perspectives can emerge over:

- Leadership styles or priorities
- Management preferences
- Strategies or processes
- Budget or financial management choices
- Decision-making approaches
- Hiring decisions, and so on

Additionally, on a broader level this list can be expanded to include:

- Political perspectives
- Religious perspectives
- Lifestyle choices
- Financial choices
- Parenting priorities and styles

I'm not suggesting that every perspective is equally valid or true. Just as you can't market however you want and expect identical results, you can't lead or relate to people however you want and expect that all your leadership or relationship efforts will work well.

What I'm suggesting is that taking time to understand what someone else's perspective is, along with how they arrived at that perspective, often worthwhile. At a minimum, it communicates that you're willing to value and offer respect to the other person, even if you don't agree with them. Additionally, taking time to understand someone else offers insight into what really motivates and drives others.

I recently received a request to help with a serious dispute between two business partners. Let's call them Nancy and John. Nancy had contacted me to ask for help. Communication had completely broken down. She couldn't get John to respond to e-mails, calls, or even a letter from her attorney. I reached out to John. He was willing to mediate, but wanted me to meet his wife first. His wife quickly made it clear she didn't trust me. Her tone was abrasive. And, as she spoke to her husband, John, she kept using the phrase, "How do we know that he is legit?" as she referred to me.

It's easy to feel frustrated in a situation like this. Nancy and John had already agreed to meet. Now, this agreement was being undermined by a third party—John's wife. My legitimacy was openly being questioned.

Instead of defending myself, I acknowledged her perspective. I validated her point, voicing that I was, indeed, a stranger to her and there was no reason to automatically trust me. I continued to discover her perspective with questions like, "What is it that you would need to see, or experience, to feel like I was legit?" I wasn't volunteering to do a "song and dance." But, I wanted to hear what was hidden underneath.

Her answer was surprising. It had nothing to do with me at all. John's wife began to spill stories of how Nancy had violated her trust. What she really wanted was to know that Nancy's offer to mediate was in good faith, and that the costs of the mediation would be fairly shared. Turns out, she wasn't challenging me at all. Defensiveness on my part would likely have delegitimized me.

By discovering and exploring her perspective (without needing to agree or disagree with it), I could get to the heart of the matter. This allowed me to target my response accurately. Within minutes, I was able to gain trust and end months of avoidance and poor communication.

My takeaway: I wouldn't have known where to press or explore if she hadn't challenged me personally. Because she created a conflict with me, I was able to identify an opportunity to dig deeper and start to uncover what was really bothering her. The new language she used, describing her concerns about Nancy, was very different than the initial language and tone she directed toward me.

If I had seen this conflict as something I needed to avoid, defend against, or win, I would never have been able to help them. By viewing conflict as an opportunity, I sensed her emotion and attack would potentially open doors to the real issue. By exploring it, as opposed to trying to overcome, I was able to discover and address the source of her concerns.

Discovering the Source: The Headwaters of Conflict

A headwater is the source of a river. If you want to understand the nature of a river, it helps to track it back to its source—the headwaters. Most often, at the source, water is pure. However, as it travels to its destination, sometimes it becomes contaminated.

While we were still newlyweds, my wife, Marta, was finishing up graduate school. It had been a dark, dreary winter followed by a rainy, miserable spring. One morning, I awakened, got quietly out of bed (so as not to disturb my wife who had been up all night working on a paper) and went to make breakfast. I stepped out of our darkened bedroom into a house that was flooded with sunlight. Immediately my spirits lifted! (It's amazing the impact weather can have on emotions.) I felt so happy; I couldn't help but want to share it with my wife.

I ran back into our bedroom, bent over her as she slept and gave her a kiss. Immediately, and unexpectedly, she turned, gave me the stink eye, and elbowed me out of the way. Then, she rolled back over to go back to sleep.

My heart dropped like a rock. A string of thoughts ran through my head. "Who is this person I married?" "What have I committed myself to?" "Is this what I'll have to deal with the rest of my life?"

I felt rejected, disappointed, embarrassed, angry, and even scared about our future together. Leaving the bedroom, I picked up my cereal bowl and went to the darkest corner of our living room. I ate angrily amidst my stormy thoughts.

Soon, Marta got up and began her day. As she walked past me on her way to the kitchen she asked, "Are you OK?"

"Yes," I answered. Sullenly.

I was stuck.

Keep in mind, this happened *after* I began my journey into dealing with conflict more effectively. So, as I was sitting there, a PowerPoint slide (Figure 1.1) I used for trainings started to flash across my mind. I knew where it was leading.

That made me even more upset.

I was sure my wife was wrong. Wasn't she the one who couldn't receive affection and ruined a sunny morning? (Never mind that she had only been asleep for a precious few hours.) I was now emotionally committed to her being wrong. I was afraid that if I looked at what was going on within me, I might end up changing my perspective on her "wrongness." And I wasn't prepared for that.

I began to think it through. I was clearly *acting out*. (I preferred to think that *she* was the one who had acted out; but I admitted I was, too.) I had made several snap *judgments*; not only about her, but also about our future marriage. I judged her and decided she was unappreciative, rejecting, and likely a poor choice as a mate.

I began to get nervous. Anyone who knows my wife knows that she is a very thoughtful and kind person. She often serves as my social legitimizer. It wasn't possible or even probable that she was as awful as I had judged her to be.

I began to think back to what it was I wanted from her. What was it that I had *demanded*? Nothing wrong, of course. I thought, "How awful is a kiss?"

But, what about when a kiss isn't reciprocated? I had demanded she respond to me (despite that she was sleeping soundly) with warmth, openness, and joy. Actually, I demanded she make me feel good.

Figure 1.1 The progression of conflict

This is exactly where the confusion so frequently begins. It begins with a *desire*.

All I desired was to share my joy about a sunny morning. Perhaps even increase my joy through sharing it. There's nothing wrong with that. In fact, there's nothing wrong about most core desires.

The problem comes when we begin to demand that someone else meet our desires.

What Are Our Core Desires?

Most of our core desires can probably be lumped into one of three categories:

Significance: I want to be valued. I want to be respected by my family, my friends, and community. I want to be appreciated. I want my work to have meaning. I want to feel like I matter.

Security: I want to feel safe physically, financially, relationally, and professionally. I want the sense of peace that comes with not needing to worry about paying the bills or the health of a loved one. I want to feel confident in the affections of my wife and the future of my career.

Satisfaction: I want the good life. I want to wake up and be happy that I've awakened next to my wife. I want to feel content with my house, be at peace in my relationships, look forward to going to work, even enjoy getting into my car.

These are good things. There's nothing wrong with desiring any of these things. However, when we perceive a threat to our ability to gain, or retain, any one of these core desires, we tend to react. That reaction can look many ways. For me, on that particular morning, I wanted to share my satisfaction in life with my wife. Even more so, being newly married, I still needed affirmation of my significance to her. And that played on my sense of security in the relationship.

That morning kiss was loaded with symbolic meaning. I had required, even demanded, that her response (despite being awakened from a dead sleep) should make me feel important, safe, and happy. If she couldn't do that, then I was perfectly justified in my pout. My withdrawal from her was beyond reproach. In fact, it was a moral high ground.

Do you see what happens? I confused good desires with unhealthy/unhelpful demands. When our desires are threatened, we shift to a position of making demands. (Even if the demand is unspoken, as in my story.) People respond to our demands because that's what they see or feel. They often don't know our desires.

We might not even know how to articulate our desires.

Our desires are the headwaters of conflict. They are the springs from which these stories flow. In most cases the source, or spring, is pure and clean. But just because water is pure at the source doesn't mean it can't quickly become polluted as it travels downstream. When we ignore our demands, judgments and acting out to defend the "purity" of our desires, it often exaggerates and accelerates conflict.

That's what makes it so confusing. When I defend my actions to my wife, she responds to my demands, my judgments, or how I'm acting out. I, on the other hand, defend my desires. Because I see my desires as pure, I insist that anything that follows is pure, as well.

Fun Houses with Scary Clowns: Experience, Perspective, and Emotions

This isn't a book on psychology, but psychology is a big part of the topic. Conflict, for most people, is an emotional experience. In many situations, what we are responding to isn't the situation itself. Instead, we're responding to what we *perceive* is happening.

New advancements in our understanding of the brain help us understand this at a deeper level. We now know that ingrained or conditioned behavior is developed by one of two different kinds of experiences. The first is a high level of repetition. The second is intense emotional experiences. Either way our brain literally adapts itself, physically, to those experiences (McEwen and Morrison 2017).

Conflict is regularly experienced as intensely emotional. As a result, our interpretation and responses to conflict can be hardwired into our brains. We have experienced conflict since we were born. We observed and experienced it in our families as we grew. We've created new families or significant relationships. We've entered the workforce, bought homes, and gained neighbors. Thousands of experiences, often emotional, some traumatic, have conditioned our understanding and experience of conflict.

When I was 21, I helped lead a team of volunteers to serve in an orphanage near Cairo, Egypt. There were some families with young children who were a part of this volunteer group. One day I was in the play area of the orphanage working with one of the men on our team. We were sifting cat droppings out of the children's sandbox. (I wanted to buy new sand. The orphanage staff just laughed at the idea of buying sand in Egypt.) So, we filtered the sand through a screen and cleaned it out the best we could. The man's 9-year-old son was playing nearby—sometimes helping, sometimes not, as kids do. At one point, the child did something that made his father angry. The man yelled at his son with a tone and energy that I recognized from my own experience growing up. Both his son and I shrank back. I felt afraid and began to emotionally recoil into myself.

While I was reacting, I remember thinking, "Wait a minute, I'm actually in charge here. I'm the leader!" So, I pulled myself out of the recoiled place I had gone and began to redirect our work into a more productive direction. It took a while to shake off the emotion of the moment and recognize the anger wasn't directed at me.

Do you see what happened?

Usually our early lessons of conflict are powerfully and emotionally charged. They were often lessons of loss, or victory, of shame, or conquest. For some of us, these lessons may have been particularly traumatic. In most cases, for most of us, we learned that conflict was *bad*. Conflict was *a threat*. Conflict was *the end*.

So now, when a colleague at work makes an odd comment to us, or a partner in a project makes an unexpected choice, or an employee disagrees with us publicly, or a spouse is impatient, it often taps into the history and emotions of experiences past.

Because of this emotional history, we're often not responding to the situation before us. More often, subconsciously, we're responding to the last time we experienced something similar.

We might not be alone in doing this. Whomever we're in conflict with may be reacting to something or someone else as well.

Figure 1.2 Cycle of Conflict

Have you ever been stuck in an argument or relationship that just goes "round and round"? Here's what's going on (See Figure 1.2):

- *Something Happens*: The event can be anything. My wife doesn't return my kiss. Someone cuts me off in traffic. A client makes a complaint. An employee makes a mistake. Actually, something doesn't even need to happen. I just need to think something *might* happen. I've experienced times where I was so sure that someone would disappoint me that it felt like they already had.

- *I React and Interpret*: There is an immediate emotional response. Even for the thinkers among us, we feel first and rationalize later. I might feel rejected, angry, and scared. Now that I'm emotionally engaged in the situation, everything feels deeply real. It doesn't matter what information I actually have; my interpretation feels so real I don't question it. Whatever

I feel, I experience as a threat to my ability to achieve or retain a sense of significance, security, or satisfaction. At the most basic level, I switch into flight, fight, or freeze mode.

This can be observed now through brain imaging. For most people in conflict, the part of the brain responsible for critical thinking, problem solving, and moral judgments turns off. The part of the brain responsible for survival, simultaneously, lights up like a Christmas tree. While this might be helpful when I encounter a bear in the forest, it's usually not helpful at a conference table or worksite.

- *I Judge*: My interpretation: She made me feel bad. My judgment: She is bad. It doesn't matter what information I have; my interpretation feels so real I don't question it. Judgment comes easily, even automatically. Usually our judgment is negative: fear or anger based. It's interesting that we rarely judge others of best intentions!

   It's human nature to feel a need to explain things. Since we now have an interpretation and judgment, we need context to make sense of it all. So, we build a story that ties it all together. Based upon our interpretation and judgment, our story makes complete sense to us.

- *We Find Supporting Evidence*: In the kiss story, I had to search for historical evidence. In many other situations, I wait until the person does something more that proves my hypothesis was correct. It's well documented that people, even researchers, tend to ignore facts that don't fit our predetermined "story;" even if we have to ignore 100 examples of how our story might be wrong.

   This phenomenon is so common that it is called a "confirmation bias." We only recognize as true what we've already believed to be true. Our stories can *feel* so true to us that it can be very difficult to let them go. We become emotionally invested in them. Even in the light of information that conflict with our initial judgments or conclusions.

   This is why reading conspiracy theories can be so interesting. Conspiracy theorists generally have mountains of detailed evidence to support their theories. In fact, the more extreme and less tenable the theory is, the longer the website and list of "facts" usually becomes.

There is never a shortage of evidence available when we're emotionally invested in a judgment.

- *Something Happens (again)*: This might be the supporting evidence mentioned above. It might be the exception, which proves the rule. Whatever it is, it sends us back into, "Here we go again!" As opposed to responding to the actual situation before us, we default back to our previous interpretations and judgments. We drag up the laundry list of complaints and examples.

We come into the conversation preloaded with emotion, assumptions, and conclusions. This is a damaging and an ineffective response pattern with someone whom we have a relationship with. It's also very easy to project all of this onto a type of person. This is a type whom we've already had an experience, made a judgment, built a story, and found our evidence. We may never have even met the specific person before; but, because they represent that type, it becomes our truth.

We create a "story," for example, about liberals or conservatives; this ethnicity or that; men or women; this department or that department; labor or management; new hires versus old-timers. We dump our story onto an unsuspecting representative of the type.

Not surprisingly, that universally fails to be received well.

Hope: Making Conflict User-Friendly

When I tell people what I do and that I have expertise in conflict resolution, I usually get two different responses. The first is, "Wow, that's great! That's really needed." The second is, "How do you handle all of that? How do you manage all the intensity and negative emotions?"

My answer to that is easy: I have hope for all my clients. I've watched so many situations resolve well that I don't worry or focus on where things appear to be right now. I focus on where they could be. And I have a very good reason for this hope.

Nearly everyone calls me as a last resort. Things are about as bad as they can imagine. Nearly everyone tells me, "We've tried everything, and it won't work." I nod and listen, and ask them a few questions regarding why they've come to that conclusion.

I also know that nearly all of them will successfully resolve the dispute. If the dispute is within an organization, the organization will nearly always be stronger as a result. Leaders and teams are often more mature and self-aware. I still receive feedback regarding disputes I helped resolve years ago. I'm told of the ongoing ripple effects of positive change and growth that continue to take place in their organizations.

So, I have hope. I have great hope.

I also have hope because I personally use what I am presenting to you. My conflicts are not fewer. In fact, now that I no longer avoid them, I probably experience more conflict. But, the nature and quality of those conflicts has dramatically and tangibly improved. They aren't prolonged, they don't have the same sense of threat, and they increasingly feel more respectful. There's a stronger sense of understanding that emerges. In fact, there's often more trust and confidence built as a result of having walked through a conflict with someone.

My wife and I still experience disagreements and conflict. She's a counselor. I'm a consultant and mediator. "People professionals" can be hypocritical at times. Not only do we know that the other person is wrong, but we also know how each other is processing improperly and communicating insufficiently.

So, we still argue at times. However, our arguments resolve more quickly now. They result in a deeper understanding about her desires and my desires. We understand more about how we both experience each other. Our conflicts help us grow.

They might even be the best thing for us.

Because we've had so many conflicts and because we've worked through them, it mitigates the sense of threat, fear, or anger. She and I both know a solution exists. In the midst of conflict, we both believe we'll eventually feel good about each other; and that these feelings will probably happen sooner rather than later. Because of that hope, even if we're acting momentarily emotional and irrational, we push forward until we've found each other again.

Now, I'm not a "Pollyanna." I don't believe everything works out for the best. I don't believe talking, listening, and understanding fix everything. I've spent time in seven different conflict zones. I've lost friends. I do believe there are some people who are just unreasonable, mean, or evil.

But those are dramatic exceptions, not the rule. The rule is most people would rather work things out; they just don't know how. They don't have hope. So, they just try to survive. They react by freezing, fleeing, or fighting.

But, you are different. You're reading this book, which means you're open to hope. By doing so, you have a profound opportunity to change your life. And, as this book is targeting leaders, you have an opportunity to create a different future for those you influence.

That's really my hope. I target leaders because we are the shapers of experience, opportunity, and meaning in our workplaces and communities. The way leaders like you and I choose to see and relate to conflict has a direct impact on how others experience and then see conflict.

Most people have never experienced conflict as a positive event. Their entire life story may be reason enough to believe that conflict is always threatening and dangerous. As leaders, it's important that we change that perception.

In the next chapters we'll dig into:

- How conflict can be good and even important for you and those you lead
- How you can learn effectively to relate to conflict
- Practical steps you can take to lead others, and transform those you lead, through the experience of conflict

I have numerous clients who have grown better and stronger as organizations because of conflict. Those leaders are more empathic and humble. Those businesses are more profitable. Those nonprofits are measurably more effective at pursuing their missions.

You, as a leader, not only can experience conflict differently, but you also can change how those around you experience conflict. You can make conflict feel safer. You can turn it into a constructive experience. You can discover how it makes your organizations healthier, more creative, and more robust than ever before.

You'll discover that conflict can actually become user-friendly. You'll do this by authentically and openly exploring your own responses and reactions. As you and I become better at relating to conflicts ourselves, it will become safer for people to relate to us. We'll begin to provide new experiences of healthy and productive conflict for others.

CHAPTER 2

Conflict Is Good: Why You Want It

Mining for Gold

I remember the first time I found gold. I was about 10 years old. It was in a steep alpine valley in Alaska. A crystal clear, cold mountain river tumbled over gravel and grey river rock.

A gold mine allowed visitors to pan for gold down river from the real mining operation. It was exciting! I had a gold pan, rubber boots, a shovel, and I was ready to go! It was hard, slow work digging the gravel and panning it out. But when the first gold flake sparkled in my pan… Wow! I was rich!

Actually, I didn't get rich. In fact, I didn't find any more gold. But even as young as I was, I could see that others were finding meaningful amounts of gold. They understood how to read the geology better than I did. They had better tools and better techniques with those tools. I realized that this was something I could get better at if I wanted to.

Investing in Growth

Mining for the opportunity in conflict is like mining for gold. You have to dig through a lot of mud and rocks until you eventually find those valuable nuggets. Sometimes you have to brave some pretty harsh conditions. Remembering the gold is there makes the work worthwhile. Additionally, the better we learn to read our situations, learn the tools, and adopt techniques that make conflict resolution possible, the more we'll be able to gain from conflicted experiences.

Fool's Gold

One lesson I learned early on is that there is something called Fool's Gold. This is a rock called pyrite. It looks similar to gold and definitely more plentiful. It initially feels good when you first find it in your pan. But it's worthless.

There are two kinds of Fool's Gold when we talk about conflict, particularly in our role as leaders. The first is a thin and temporary sense of peace that comes from avoiding issues or denying that they are there. The second is the pyrrhic sense of victory that comes with winning a conflict, particularly when that win comes at the cost of relationship, credibility, or internal peace.

Real Gold

This is what real gold looks like: *True gold is insight into the heart and minds of yourself and those you lead.* Conflict exposes the presence of deeply held desires or interests. This is the level where all human motivation is rooted. The ability to work and relate at this level is what separates the best leaders from everyone else.

Finding Real Gold: Four Opportunities

There are four primary spheres where conflict occurs within any organization. This chapter explores the opportunities, or gold, hidden in each.

Every organization is made up of four different components: people, relationships, structures, and culture. You can't remove any one of these components and expect the organization to last long.

The Four Opportunity Lens

Conflict is an amazing opportunity for people, and leaders, in particular, to grow. As a consultant, I use the Four Opportunity Lens to diagnose the sources of conflict and where the opportunities for growth lie. The Four Opportunity Lens examines the four basic components of every organizational dynamic: personal responses, relational responses, organizational structure, and organizational culture (See Figure 2.1).

Each of these translates into an opportunity for growth:

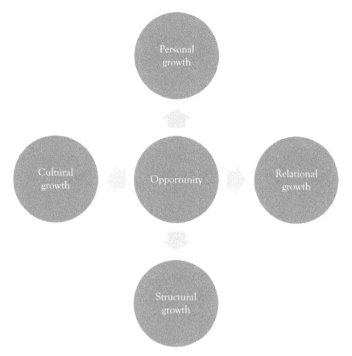

Figure 2.1 Four Opportunities Lens

The First Opportunity: Personal Growth

Conflict is an opportunity to cultivate our own personal maturity and development. Because conflict is a stressor, it triggers emotions. We tend to have a less-filtered response to our emotions when stressed. Think of these strong emotions like you think of an automobile's "check engine light." In and of themselves, they don't communicate much. However, exploring how we interpret, relate to, and respond to conflict opens a window for deep insight into personal issues and opportunities for repair.

When a conflict occurs, it exposes our gut level beliefs and responses. If we are open to it, this helps us discover underlying behaviors and mindsets that may not be serving us well.

When I teach conflict resolution to groups I often lead out with an exercise. (You can do this with me right now.) Here is the exercise:

Think of a current or very recent conflict that you've experienced. Think of the people that were involved. Give the conflict or situation a name.

In your mind's eye, drift back in your memory to the point where you first realized that there was a conflict. What was the feeling that you felt?

I've done this exercise with many different groups in several countries. Two things are consistent:

1. Everyone has a current conflict to refer to.
2. Almost all the words that come from the groups sound like: angry, sad, scared, sick, frustrated, nauseous, disappointed, shocked, discouraged, anxious, tired, and so on.

What this demonstrates is no shock to anyone. We almost universally experience conflict as a negative event.

However, we don't tend to think beyond this. Why is a disagreement, a misunderstanding, a strongly expressed emotion so threatening to me? Typically, this is because of the thousands of experiences starting in childhood where any conflict we experienced typically meant the end of something: the end of a relationship; the end of an opportunity; the end of a good time; and the end of "normal."

It doesn't take long before we believe at an instinctive level that conflict is bad and something to either avoid or quickly win.

But those two approaches don't work well. We learn that over time as well. The bully often doesn't go away just because we ignore him or her. Using a baseball bat to even the odds with the bully lands us in worse trouble.

This is particularly true in situations where we have ongoing relationships with the people we have conflict with. What value is there in *winning* an argument with my wife if I've pushed her farther from me? What value is there in *winning* an argument with an employee, colleague, or customer if they feel devalued as a result?

If it were so much better to just avoid dealing with the issue, why does avoidance tend to create toxic workplaces? The avoided issues (perhaps an ethical or safety situation, an employee or department not pulling their weight, a caustic employee who is always complaining and gossiping about others) can be expected to result in one or more of the following:

1. We lose our better, more confident people who know they have options elsewhere.
2. We suck the morale, drive, and energy out of our people so that subperformance becomes the norm.
3. We wait until someone (perhaps us) finally has had it, blows up and deals with the situation in a way that may easily create at least as much damage as good. While it helps to avoid *causing* a conflict, that isn't the same thing as avoiding addressing an existing conflict. Even if that conflict is staying quiet for the time being. As leaders, it doesn't help us grow, help improve employee or customer relationships, or build more structurally sound or culturally robust workplaces.

Conflict causes reactions. Reactive leadership is not the most effective leadership. However, significant growth is possible if we decide to utilize the experience of conflict as an exercise in self-discovery and self-awareness. If we relate to each conflict we encounter as an experiment: "How can I listen better?" "How can I put aside my defensiveness?" "Why do I feel like this complaint is a personal attack?" We can become far more effective and insightful in our leadership.

A simple tool for growth is to ask the following questions following a conflicted situation. Try to answer them as objectively and honestly as possible.

- What happened?
- What was my contribution? (What did I do or say? What was my attitude?)
- What was I trying to accomplish?
- What was the result?
- What have I learned?
- What might I do differently?

The Second Opportunity: Relational Growth

Conflict is an opportunity to build trust in relationships. It can provide insight into how to engage with the motivations of others.

Relational trust is built by experiencing patterns over time. If a coworker shuts down and stops talking whenever there is a conflict, trust breaks down. Others may develop a sense that they are walking on egg shells around this person.

However, if a coworker stays in the conversation and works through it with us, trust is built. We know this person can be relied on when things get tense. The behaviors demonstrated during conflict are a powerful insight into character.

Don't miss this: *There is no opportunity to build this level of trust outside of conflict.* I'll go into this in much more detail in later chapters. But here are some of the key elements of the opportunities in relationship.

Conflict creates Stress. Stress creates growth. In the human body, we are only able to build our strength, our stamina, our sense of balance and agility and our cardio vascular system when we stress ourselves. It's just enough stress to create growth. We can condition ourselves to handle more physical stress (lifting more, running further) without it being any more overwhelming.

We literally build our muscles, our bones, our heart, our vasculature, our brain and our full nervous system when we stress ourselves. If there is too much stress we end up injured. If there is never time to recover, we end up fatigued or injured. But if we are deconditioned and there is little or no stress, we atrophy. We shrink. We develop fragility. We become less nimble and agile.

In relationships, there is a corollary. Engaging in challenging conversations and situations helps our relationship grow. Not enough challenge (too much passivity and avoidance) and our actual relationship shrinks. It becomes fragile. It isn't nimble or agile.

If there is too acute of a challenge in a relationship—such as when trust or safety is violated or if challenge is too frequent and constant, relational injury often occurs.

If our relationships are "deconditioned" what might feel like a normal conversation to one person may feel like an attack to someone else. Who is right? It really doesn't matter—what does matter is the "conditioning" of the relationship—where there is sufficient trust and ability by all involved to engage in the conversation.

Conflict exposes what is really important: I'll go into much greater detail on this later. What's valuable to keep in mind is that people only put energy into a conflict when something matters to them. However, *what* it is that matters is often a little mysterious. Sometimes even to ourselves.

When conflict occurs it demonstrates that what matters to one or more people is closer to the surface and feels threatened. We can often learn a lot about those in our relationships when we start to understand what is really important to them. It's rare that this kind of information surfaces in normal workplace conversations because it may feel too intimate for a collegial relationship. Or the conversations just never go in that direction. But these things will emerge during a conflict.

As we learn more about each other's values and expectations and desires—we're able to relate with each other more effectively. We know how to respect each other's differences *and* we learn that we may share commonalities we weren't aware of.

As Leaders We Can Create New Patterns Through Conflict. Human behavior change usually happens through repetition or an intensely emotional experience. Conflict is very emotional for many people. In some environments, it is also common or repeatedly encountered.

As leaders, we can use this opportunity to help our colleagues and those we supervise to learn new patterns of behavior. This primarily happens through modeling the techniques and skills I'll introduce in this book.

When people experience our leadership in a conflict they are impacted. They are coming to us from their own backgrounds and histories. If, when they experience us in conflict and it feels respectful, truthful and safe (even if also intense and difficult) and the conversation leads to genuine resolution—we actually start to reshape their ability to relate to others. On a very literal level, this can begin to rewire how people see and interpret life. It opens up new opportunities for them. It grows them. This grows our teams.

The Third Opportunity: Structural Growth

Structural Growth: Nearly all information on conflict resolution focuses on the personal and relational aspects of conflict. However, many workplace conflicts are created or inflamed by organizational structures.

Just as a conflict provides us with personal and relational insights, it also provides insight into the structures and systems we operate within. Some policies support good communication. Others impede it. Some procedures improve decision making and relationships. Others weaken them. Sometimes, even the physical space where we work creates more psychological safety and improves collaboration. Other times, it puts our safety at risk and encourages silos to form.

On more the one occasion I've worked with groups who've spent years stuck on an issue—only to help them resolve it in a matter of hours. The issue? They weren't sure how to structure a conversation for that particular topic.

In the workplace, it's very common for structural issues to be the core contributor to ongoing, regular conflicts. These are usually misdiagnosed as personal issues or relationship problems; because that is often how they manifest. However, the underlying issues are often due to organizational structures or the lack thereof.

And that is the challenge. The structural issues, themselves, aren't always obvious or visible. (Who can see the "lines of authority?") Additionally, it is commonly the place that the structures that helped build a very successful organization no longer serve it well. The entrepreneurial nimbleness that may have been required may be undermining a contemporary need for stability and predictability. Or vice versa.

Many entrepreneurial, privately held companies tend to be under structured. Then, when they run into a series of conflicts or internal "disasters" they often create reactionary structure. The scars of these past conflicts are often quickly evident in the organization's bylaws or policy documents. These reactionary structures are almost never designed to help the organization be as successful in its purpose as it can be or as health as it can be. They are nearly always designed to make sure that "*that* never happens again."

Organizations that experience more regulatory scrutiny (such as publicly held corporations, health care organizations, government entities, etc.) tend to be far more risk and liability aware. Again, their structures are often more designed to protect them from liability than from achieving their purpose or creating an ideal place to work.

Not that avoiding liability isn't important. But no organization was ever formed purely for the purpose of avoiding liability. The structure should serve the purpose of the organization, which includes the overall operational health of the organization.

That, on its own, mitigates liability.

This is so true and common that I will no longer engage in a workplace intervention if I'm not allowed to examine workplace structures. To not explore and address potential structural drivers of conflict is just play a game of whack-a-mole with conflict.

The Fourth Opportunity: Cultural Growth

Conflict exposes the powerful beliefs and values that create our organizational cultures. These are the things that invisibly shape our entire experience and understanding. Many cultures have a low tolerance for, or fear of conflict. Conflict is often symbolic of things going very badly, or wrong. For some, this belief is so deep that conflict can be equated with "wrongness" or "sinfulness." Frequently this creates a pattern of avoidance or denial until problems have grown out of control. There might be very passive-aggressive reactions to conflict. Or there might be a determined avoidance until someone or something explodes.

Other cultures may have a strong sense that authority must never be questioned. It's not that conflict shouldn't exist but conflict should never exist with someone in authority. Over time, a leader ends up being surrounded by, "Yes Men and Women." If there is a choice, the healthiest people tend to leave and go elsewhere. Particularly if they have leadership potential. This means that the organization becomes full of people who tend toward being compliant, avoid standing out, and won't speak up if there is a problem. Eventually, these habits make it difficult to grow leadership from within.

Some cultures promote the idea that only the strongest survive. Conflict is an opportunity to weed out the weak, the disloyal, or the dissenters. The organization may frame this differently, for example by focusing on the benefits of competition. However, if everyone is focused on competition (which is often a synonym for survival) and no one is focused on being a team—the organization will silo. People and teams will start to look more to their own interests then the interests of the whole.

All of these cultural approaches take a heavy toll on the organization. Many organizations are so accustomed to bearing the weight or cost of unhealthy conflict that they don't believe (and can be difficult to convince) that any other reality is possible. The surprising reality is that shifting how an organization relates to conflict is one of the easiest ways to grow a bottom line.

Similar to structure, addressing how culture impacts relationships, communication and trust is critical to developing lasting solutions. While culture change can feel nebulous it is actually very malleable—for leaders. Of all of the four opportunities, culture change becomes the area that has the widest, most far reaching and sustainable impact.

Using the Four Opportunities Lens

Each of the four lenses provides insight and options for the leader. I'll explore each at greater depth later in the book.

I encourage leaders to begin by looking at their own personal responses to conflict and their relationships first. Then to begin looking at how their behaviors and the values and perspectives that those behaviors reflect are shaping the culture of their teams or organizations. Systems and structures should then be designed to help the support the ideal culture that you are building.

There is no linear process through all of this. Just like if someone decides to become physically fit, they don't first sleep well for a week, then eat well for a week, then start working out for a week. It all happens at the same time. They are all dependent on each other. There will be ebbs and flows in your focus in each area depending on what you are trying to accomplish and the needs of the moment.

If you grow in your ability to relate to conflict, you'll discover an increased confidence and effectiveness when addressing difficult conversations.

If you work on your relationships, you'll discover that your credibility will grow.

If you work on structures, you'll find that the frequency of unnecessary conflicts will diminish.

If you work on culture, you'll create a workplace that is resilient and self-healing.

CHAPTER 3

The Primary Sources of Conflict: It Ain't About Chemistry

Before trying to resolve a conflict, it is useful to understand what is causing it. Many conflicts are prolonged or inflamed, even when we make good faith efforts to resolve them, because we have misdiagnosed the cause of the conflict.

To begin, it is helpful to understand that all conflicts can be broken down into two basic types: *Substantive* and *Personal.*

Substantive conflicts are about how something is done, about the goals you want to achieve, about values that you believe should guide behavior, or about the information that people have. They are generally external to the people involved in the conflict. In many cases they are easy to identify. However, in the case of values, it can take more insight to pinpoint the source. In the case of information, it can take time to realize that not everyone has the same set of data.

Personal conflicts are about character and relationships. They are internal to the people involved. They frequently revolve around whether someone trusts or feels respected or liked by others. They range from the tension that can emerge from experiences that can include:

- Not being able to trust someone. Or not feeling trusted.
- Not feeling respected. Or struggling to respect someone.
- Believing that not everyone on your team can be trusted to pull their own weight.
- Someone who is controlling and demanding.
- When your opinions or concerns aren't heard.

- Personal issues might be difficult to identify if they haven't been communicated; or if someone isn't willing to acknowledge them.

As we explore these two, it is helpful to remember:

- It is easy for a substantive conflict to become personalized, particularly if the people involved tend to view all conflict as being personal.
- It is easy for personal conflict to impact substantive issues. Often a substantive issue will take on symbolic power that is primarily fueled by the personal conflict.
- Both kinds of conflict, when expressed in a healthy way, can be an important and very valuable part of team building as well as organizational health and success.

It's Not About You: Substantive Conflicts

Substantive conflict tends to be about four different things: disagreements about outcomes, process, values, or data.

It's About *What*: Outcomes

Many conflicts are about two or more sides who feel that the other is preventing them from getting or keeping something they want. This is the most obvious source of conflict. This is frequently where most people tend to focus. Examples of this are obvious and easily relatable:

- One partner wants to hire someone. The other partner doesn't.
- An employee wants a raise. The employer says, "No."
- A supervisor assigns a new responsibility. The employee chooses to ignore it.
- The buyer wants to pay as little as possible for a business. The seller wants to earn as much as possible.

Each of these scenarios opens the door to the classic *zero-sum* solution. In other words, a solution where if someone wins, someone else necessarily loses. This is a compelling and easily grasped perspective. It can also be enormously inflammatory.

One of the basic theoretical frameworks in the field of sociology is called, "Conflict Theory." This theory describes one of the most common ways people interpret human interactions. In short, Conflict Theory suggests that for one person or group to win or gain, someone else will need to lose. This perspective is frequently flipped—if one person or group feels like they are losing, they believe that this is happening due to someone else's gain.

This is powerfully compelling perspective. It can stir up tremendous passions. In fact, it is frequently used to do just that.

It's also an overly simple way to explain human interaction. While it can offer explanations of conflict that are emotionally satisfying, it rarely paints the full picture.

It's helpful to keep exploring. To see if there are alternative or multi-causal explanations that do a better job of helping us diagnose what is happening.

It's About *How*: Process

Disputes often emerge due to *how* a decision is made or carried out. The best facilitators of change processes are acutely aware that they need to execute *how* well.

In 2001, I was 27 and involved in my first humanitarian disaster. I worked in Kosovo, as a part of the international relief effort after the NATO intervention. Eighty percent of the homes where I worked had been damaged or destroyed during the ethnic war between the Serbs and the ethnic Albanians.

I worked for Medair, one of the two agencies conducting the bulk of the reconstruction effort. The majority of my time was focused on overseeing the reconstruction effort in 15 communities. I was responsible for everything from the initial assessment and beneficiary identification process to overseeing the construction process to completion.

This seemed like a great opportunity to really help a lot of people. However, I learned that helping well takes more thoughtfulness, discipline, and skill than I originally thought.

At the end of the project, I was tasked with completing a beneficiary assessment. So, I traveled to every community and tried to meet with every family that we had served to receive their feedback. It became an uncomfortable task.

In my memory, this boils down to a single conversation I had with one family. It was late November, cold and snowy out. I sat inside their warm, newly rebuilt home. After going through the traditional rituals of greetings and coffee, we began talking. Initially the husband thanked me, told me they were grateful; everything was very good.

But things didn't feel very good. There was an unspoken tension. Part of me was hoping we'd just wrap up the conversation and I could go.

Then the wife spoke up. Her words drilled down inside me.

"We are very grateful for Medair and your work and your help. We wouldn't be here if it weren't for you. But the way you helped us hurt."

Our goal was good. Our intent was good.

But that wasn't enough.

She elaborated briefly. Our process, or at least the part I was responsible for, was clumsy and created problems for them and conflict within the community. It was hard to listen to what she was saying. I wanted to defend our work based on my desire ("But we wanted to help!"). I felt tempted to judge her ("We're sitting in the nice, warm home that we gave you. Ingrate!").

Fortunately, I just listened. As I did, I began to gain insight into the challenges we experienced in many of the communities we had served.

The way we conducted the assessment process stirred up rivalries, jealousies, and conflict within each community. The way we conducted the selection process became a tool that some local leaders used against each other to strengthen their power base and create factions. The way we oversaw the construction process and our timetable created additional stresses on already overtaxed families.

In short, although we came to do good, the way we did it created conflict.

I went back and reviewed the initial project plans. I discovered they were very thoughtfully designed and addressed all the issues discussed. The problem wasn't the original plan or intent. It was *how* we actually implemented those plans that created the problems. The rush to complete, the stress, the lack of knowledge on the part of staff, like myself, created these problems. When we deviated from a Habitat for Humanity informed *sweat equity* model of construction to whatever was fastest and easiest (for us) in terms of getting homes built, we opened the doors to fraud, conflict, and jealousy. I didn't appreciate the value of *how*.

How decisions are made in your teams, how people are or aren't included, how communication is handled, how accountability is approached matters.

Process matters.

What Is Effective Process?

When you experience conflict, and discover that process is all or part of the cause, it is important to explore what was wanted, expected, or needed by the parties concerned. This allows you to improve your process.

While what constitutes an effective process is situationally dependent, here are some common elements of effective process:

Gather Input from those Impacted

The term *stakeholders* is often used to describe all the different kinds of people who have a stake in *how* a particular decision, project, or initiative plays out. It is *very* common for ideas or projects to meet resistance because someone didn't feel involved or consulted with early on. Knowing who to involve, when, and how is a skill (and even a profession) all in itself. It helps to think of this effort as front-loading.

There can be considerable time and effort needed to develop a process that feels good or respectful to all (or as many as possible) people involved. However, this is usually far less time, effort, and cost than what is needed to bring a project to life that isn't support by stakeholders or, worse, is actively resisted.

Clear Communication

The best communication should be as clear as possible, as soon as possible, as frequently as possible, as objectively and factually as possible. When leaders do not communicate people a timely way or with sufficient information they should anticipate problems. People intend to fill the information void by making up their own version of the facts or become so disenfranchised that they stop caring.

Real-Time Feedback and Feedforward

Feedback is often looks like asking someone, "How did we do?" It's a rearview mirror on events. Creating a process to receive as much real-time feedback as possible on how the process is working allows you to identify and correct problems early.

Feedforward is a process where you ask, specifically, "What are recommendations for what we should do to improve (in the desired area)?" A feedforward process allows you to quickly guide concerns and complaints and reformat them into actionable suggestions: "How could we do this differently next time?" It allows you to capture useful information and perspectives that may not otherwise be offered.

Appropriate and Situational Exercise of Power

Not all decisions are equal, have the luxury of time, or can involve everyone. A leader's ability to primarily exercise *influence* instead of *power* will mitigate conflict. The more frequently a leader makes command decisions, the more they'll either meet resistance or disengage an audience (which creates its own kind of conflict).

Capacity for Course Correction

Some leaders function like every decision is an artillery shot. Once fired, it can't be recalled. "The decision has been made. Can't do anything about it now." This is poor leadership. Most decisions have the potential to be steered, adjusted, or corrected, particularly as new and better information becomes available. The most robust systems are strongly directed but have the capacity to course correct when needed.

Most of the work of leadership is an essay. Not a math test. Correcting and improving our decisions as we go is leadership wisdom.

Establish Decision Making Criteria in Advance

When making decisions, particularly group decisions, a powerful technique for both better decision making and avoiding conflict is to establish the qualities of an acceptable or desirable decision or decision-making process in advance. For example, let's imagine a business with two partners. When only one partner is ready to cash out and retire, conflict often emerges around the value of that person's shares in the company.

In an ideal scenario, each business's operating agreement or bylaws would spell out how this should be done in advance. Unfortunately, in most cases, these documents are poorly written or haven't been updated to be relevant. Despite this, the relationship of both partners will be best served if they agree in advance *how* the valuation and buyout process will occur before pursuing it.

For example, they discuss and agree that they want an independent and neutral perspective on the valuation of the company. They both agree that the departing owner wants to be completely separated from the future performance of the company. By identifying these underlying interests, a process that can be chosen that is less likely to provoke conflict.

They may agree to something that looks like: hiring an independent valuator and accepting the valuation that comes from that process. They decide that their buyout payment plan should not be dependent on future company performance. So, the departing partner won't self-finance. The remaining partner will either bring in new investors by a defined date or will obtain financing for a complete buyout.

It's About *Why*: Values

Because of the work that we did in Kosovo, I served on the Regional Housing Committee. This was a governmental committee, under the auspices of the United Nations (UN), that oversaw all things housing and property related. Along with the immense amount of war-related property damage, for the previous decade while Yugoslavia was disintegrating, essentially no property records were kept. This meant that everything related to deeds, maps, boundary lines, building or health codes, water and sanitation, and more had all gone to seed. Any records that survived the war were historical. Not contemporary.

To attempt to create some sense of order, we developed a process by which all communities in the region were shared equally between our agency and a partner agency. The assignment of these communities took place within the Housing Committee. We also had a very defined and involved process for assessing the need in the communities and choosing beneficiaries. Once a community had been through either agency's process, it was considered *finished* and no longer eligible for that level of assistance. An appeals process was also in place. This system of processes generally worked effectively.

One day, I received a request to assess a single family in a village that was finished. The request came from the European Union (EU) monitor who served with me on the Regional Housing Committee. The EU was a major donor to the reconstruction effort. The monitor was a local man whose job was to ensure that we carried out our job to the specifications and intent of the EU. He had significant power because he was able to influence whether we continued to be funded.

I reminded him that our work in that village was completed. The Housing Committee had determined that there were no more families in the community that qualified for services. Additionally, there was an appeals process, if they thought we had made a mistake. He should direct his request through appropriate appeals process.

He agreed, but said that this was a unique scenario. Someone had been overlooked. Even if I said, "No" would I at least conduct an assessment?

Local staff and officials would often ask expatriates to be the public face of hard decisions. In many cases, we volunteered this as it took local pressure off our local partners. However, to tell someone, "No" was often a difficult process. It was common for the conversation ended in tears, or blame, or even personal death threats. All of that to say, I didn't like it. However, given that he was probably motivated by a cultural need to save face, I agreed.

As I began the assessment I discovered something quickly. The EU monitor had asked me to assess the home of his father and mother.

His request was a clear violation of our ethics policy. He should have recused himself from involvement in it. Not only that, they wouldn't have qualified for the program by normal standards as they already had a new house built by some other means.

I was outraged. Not only was my time being wasted but the monitor was also overtly engaging in corruption. He was using his position on the committee and as monitor to pressure me to direct resources for what was, from my perspective, personal benefit.

I talked this over with my supervisor and the head of the UN mission in that region. In those conversations, I was reminded of very different cultural values that were in conflict:

- For the EU monitor: Loyalty and duty to family were among the highest values to uphold and maintain.
- For myself: Integrity and honesty were some of the highest and most guiding values.

In a situation where he was asked to choose between family duty and integrity, his choice was obvious. His father asked him to use his position to get a home. He would do this.

For myself, the integrity of the process was paramount. I was unwilling to yield.

There was a conflict over which value was the most important value. It isn't that the EU Monitor wouldn't care if he was lied to or would say integrity was irrelevant. It isn't that I don't care about my family or loyalty to those that I care about.

But we weighted these values differently. When those values appeared to conflict with each other, we each placed different ones first. When it came to choose his battles, he decided he'd rather risk a conflict with me than risk a conflict with his family.

When diagnosing a conflict, it is very helpful to explore if there is a value conflict such as described above. Once we see this, at a minimum, it begins to open the doors to understanding. Additionally, it might help me understand that while what the EU monitor made an improper request, he likely was less interested in the request being granted than he was in being able to demonstrate to his family that he had tried and that I was the person who prevented him from helping.

It's About "What": Data

As I write this, *Fake News*, or fabricated stories that make their way into media, is a frequently discussed and stressed about phenomena. Following the presidential election in 2016, there have been many inquiries and speculations regarding the influence of Fake News on the election. Additionally, there have been instances of policy makers referencing Fake News in their decisions.

Most of the hand-wringing over Fake News is disingenuous. When I was in high school, and an editor on the student paper, the term we learned was "Yellow Journalism." This term was established in the late 1800s to address fake news reporting that disregarded any need to base itself in fact and was focused more on creating attention grabbing. This, the clickbait of the 19th century, is blamed for being a major contributor to the Spanish-American war. Before that term was coined, there were other terms. In fact, for as long as people have told the news, they have taken liberties with its veracity or made it up all together.

Thomas Jefferson, a champion of free press and a framer of first amendment language, vented his frustrations in a private letter:

> *"I deplore...the putrid state into which our newspapers have passed and the malignity, the vulgarity, and mendacious spirit of those who write for them...These ordures are rapidly depraving the public taste and lessening its relish for sound food. As vehicles of information and a curb on our functionaries, they have rendered themselves useless by forfeiting all title to belief...this has, in a great degree, been produced by the violence and malignity of party spirit."*

("Founders Online: Thomas Jefferson To Walter Jones, 2 January 1814" 2017)

My point?

Conflict is often due to or exacerbated by bad data. Faulty information. Arriving at conclusions based on incomplete or inaccurate facts.

This often creates a negative spiral. Poor data create conflict. Conflict justifies the use of or fabrication of data. One feeds the other.

When I was first learning to mediate, I quickly discovered that in nearly every case, both parties had different understandings of what the *facts* were. While there was often some element of denial, minimization, or outright lying, it was also common that the parties just had very different sets of facts that they were operating from. It has become a common part of my practice to explore what each side believes to be true.

It is only in rare cases that they will both describe a similar set of facts. In most cases, I can recognize they are describing the same situation—from different vantage points. In a few situations, I wouldn't even know we were talking about the same conflict—so divergent was the information that everyone was operating from. Over time, I began to observe that the more divergent the perspective of the facts was, the more toxic and difficult to resolve the situation was. If parties had close agreement about what happened, it was often relatively easy to help them achieve resolution.

What Is Your Evidence for That?

We protect ourselves and others when we ask for evidence. When we check the sources of information. When we take the extra effort to communicate clearly.

I've worked in many places where it is a sign of personal honor to be able to business on a handshake. To write things down, or create a contract, can be seen as a sign of distrust. However, many conflicts emerge because of differences in memory regarding what was agreed to. I learned to advise that some kind of written agreement always be established, even if this is as informal as sending an e-mail that recounted the specific details of the agreement.

It *Is* About You: Personal Conflict

One of the great challenges of substantive conflict is that it tends to become personal very easily. In the workplace, disagreements about outcomes can become personal battles judging the motivation or capacity of others. Disagreements over process can alienate and demotivate members of your team. A lack of alignment or understanding about how to relate with differing values in the workplace can erode trust and respect. Differences in data can easily lead to or be perceived as a willful avoidance of facts, jumping to conclusions, or making assumptions.

Ultimately, substantive conflicts are the easiest to resolve if they've not yet become infected with personal conflict. Substantive conflicts are often a place for healthy discussion and debate. Better answers and decisions often emerge from them—until it gets personal.

Condemned to Repeat History

Those who cannot remember the past are condemned to repeat it.

—George Santayana

History doesn't repeat itself, but it does rhyme.

—Mark Twain

My experience in Southern Sudan was a pivot point for me. This was not the first team conflict that I found myself in. In fact, when I am willing to be honest, my life has been surrounded by conflict. Some of these conflicts I caused, some I was drawn into, some I was part of the collateral damage, and some I was just a spectator to.

In every case, I didn't know what to do to turn things around. Once in a while, I was able to achieve a genuine reconciliation with someone. In even rarer circumstances, I was able to help others work through their disputes. The majority of the time, though, conflict was like getting sucked into a powerful, white water current. I would just get sucked away and pray that I made it out on the other side.

Whether history repeats or rhymes, it tends to produce similar experiences, until something changes. In Southern Sudan, I finally realized that I was the common variable in all the conflicts I had experienced. I was the only variable that I could control. I realized that the best hope I had for breaking free would be if I changed how I related to conflict.

At some level, all conflict is personal. It is all about me (or you) and how I (or you) interpret what is happening and choose to respond. There is an innate uncontrollableness about conflict. That's what makes it so terrifying for so many.

But I can learn to control myself. I can cultivate self-awareness. I no longer need to just react. If I do, I can correct my reactions earlier. I can learn perspectives for interpreting what is happening, at least on my side, so that I can better choose my next response. I can learn skills for responding in ways that make resolution more likely.

While it will always and forever remain the case that other people are often the drivers of a conflict—be they overly sensitive, reactive, insecure, arrogant, or any other number of labels that we choose—it is equally true that we will find ourselves intentionally or unintentionally in conflicts that will need to be resolved.

If you are interested in breaking free from your history of ineffectively resolved disputes, you'll need to begin to do things differently.

Earlier this year, I was involved in a conflict with a past client. I misinterpreted an e-mail he sent. Instead of calling, I made the error of e-mailing my response. I wasn't angry or out of control. But my response was very out of context. In a way that I didn't understand, my response was received as highly offensive.

It was easy to want to swing in one (or both) or two typical reactions: (1) *blame and dismiss*—to want to either interpret him as having the problem, being overly sensitive and unreasonable. To say, "good riddance" to the relationship, or (2) *capitulate and grovel*—to shotgun the apologies until I finally hit whatever it was that created the offense. To roll over on my back and do whatever it takes to make peace.

Neither response serves either of us. I genuinely did misinterpret his e-mail. I did respond more reactively than thoughtfully. To blame and dismiss his concerns robs me of the opportunity to better understand him.

To capitulate and grovel robs him of the opportunity to build a relationship of mutual trust and confidence with me. To fake peace by just trying to smooth ruffled feathers doesn't allow either of us to grow.

So, I've asked that we set aside the business aspect of our conversation. I acknowledged my part, as best as I currently understand it. I've recognized the existence of some of the other hurt and offense, without taking a false ownership. I've asked that we meet so that we can hear each other out and work toward resolution.

I've chosen, for myself, that a relationship of mutual trust and respect is more important than acquiring new business or my comfort.

I didn't know if there would be mutual understanding and reconciliation. All I could do was be humble about my errors, be willing to listen, and continue to do what I can to increase the odds of genuine reconciliation.

The process has taken time. He avoided the conversation for quite a while. Then, in part because of staff pressure to bring me back in, he's reached out to reconnect.

We're still working on this. As we look at new projects, our success will be impacted by how we address the past. We can't ignore it. It won't help to dwell on it. But it will need to be addressed. So, as I pursue clear communication and setting expectations and boundaries, I will also do so in ways that reestablish mutual trust and respect.

If I win him back over, our relationship will likely be stronger than ever for the effort. I may not win the relationship back. But I've learned that the effort is worth it, both in terms of personal peace as well as business.

Critical Ingredients: Trust, Respect, and Care

When a workplace conflict occurs, it is very difficult to resolve at a meaningful level until three different components have been established: trust, respect, and care. (Figure 3.1.)

> *Trust* refers to the degree the other party believes both that, "I mean what I say," and "I will do what I say."
>
> *Respect* refers to their belief that, "I value them personally, professionally, *and* am willing to act in ways that communicate that respect."
>
> *Care* refers to their belief that, "I care about them personally. Their happiness, their dreams, their well-being have value for me."

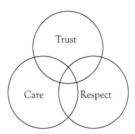

Figure 3.1 Critical relationship ingredients

Thought Experiment

Imagine a recent conflict. It might be ongoing or in the past. Identify which of the three elements were violated, never existed, or in some way were weakened. It might have been one. It might have been all three.

Let's imagine that the conflict still exists. In this imaginary scenario, you find that things have improved to the point where you do trust them. You also believe they respect and care about you.

As you imagine this, what are the behaviors they demonstrate that communicate trustworthiness, respect, or care to you?

How do these changes in behavior impact your perception of the conflict?

For more people, it lowers the sense of intensity considerably. It also provides a sense of hope that resolution could happen. In some cases, the entire conflict disappears.

If I believe that someone cares and respects me, but I don't trust them, I may tend to hold back.

If I believe someone is trustworthy and cares about me but I don't feel fully respected by them, I may feel devalued or resentful.

If I believe someone is trustworthy and respects my abilities but don't feel they care about me, I may feel manipulated.

Creating a Different Future

For most people, conflict is experienced emotionally. This is true, even if the emotional response is to shut down the emotions. This is because most people grew up associating conflict with strong negative feelings such as fear, anger, grief, or loss. These strong emotions anchor patterns of behavior into our brain. This creates a vicious cycle. We begin to fall into a very common thinking error called *confirmation bias.* This is the Cycle of Conflict discussed earlier.

The Way Out

To get out of the cycle, I have to admit where I am at in it. Then I have to try to separate what I actually know is a *fact* from what is *interpretation*. In the incident I described with the previous client, there are almost no facts regarding the other person. It is nearly all interpretation.

I need to get out of my head, go to the source (the person with whom I have an issue), and do my best to get actual information.

This takes courage. Later, I'll introduce tools that you can use for this conversation.

The Tip of the Iceberg Didn't Sink the Titanic

The concept of *underlying interests* has been around for thousands of years. However, Roger Fisher and William Ury in their classic book, *Getting to Yes* (Patton, Ury, and Fisher 2014), have helped reintroduce it into the contemporary fields of negotiation and mediation. It is a powerful and helpful concept. It helps people shift from zero-sum or intractable disputes into conversations where mutually acceptable solutions are more possible.

The basic framework of the concept looks like this (Table 3.1):

There is an *Issue*: This is what the conflict is about. Sometimes there is more than one issue. It is usually helpful to identify and address these issues separately. Just clarifying the issues often helps resolve some of the disagreement.

Beneath issues are *Positions*: Positions are the solutions that we suggest will solve the issues. Most conflicts manifest or become intractable here.

Exploration of *Interests* is nearly always missed. However, when it is addressed, it usually allows the most robust and mutually satisfactory

Table 3.1 Issues, positions, and interests

Issue (A description of the conflict)		
Positions (Person A) Person A's solutions, suggestions, or demands for resolving the issue.	**Position (Person B)** Person B's solutions, suggestions, or demands for resolving the issue.	
Interests (Person A) Underlying desires of Person A.	**Interest (Shared)** Underlying desires shared by *both* Person's A and B.	**Interests (Person B)** Underlying desires of Person B.
Options for solution A list of options that satisfies as many of both person's underlying interests as possible.		

approach to decision making. Interests are the underlying desires or needs. In many cases, there is a high level of agreement (or at least neutrality) at the level of interests.

I'm a big planner. I'm the ideal guy to travel with into a disaster zone. Plan before you go, plan again when you arrive, regularly check in, and replan. Set clear goals. Attack them. Vacations, with this nebulous objective of "relaxation," have often been challenging for me. I understand the concept of planned spontaneity. I'm not always sure how to *do* this business of relaxing.

My wife prefers to take things as they come and enjoy the journey. She vacations very naturally. She's completely content to vacation without a set of objectives. She's excellent at vacationing.

Our first couple of vacations were rough. I preferred to blame my wife for this, which, of course, helped nothing. The truth is that between the two of us, she was the only one who seemed to know how to approach a vacation.

My brother lives in New Zealand. We decided to plan a trip to visit. I decided this time, my primary objective for the trip (because I love objectives) was to try to smooth out or eliminate relational rough spots in advance. I realized I needed to approach it differently, because I generated most of the tension.

I used issues, positions, and interests to get there. (Table 3.2.)

The Issue: How do we take a trip that we both enjoy?
My Position: I wanted a low-stress trip. For me, that meant a trip that was planned out. **My Wife's Position:** She didn't want me to be stressed on the trip and ruin it.
That stressed me.

I was planning the flights, the RVs, where we would stay, the itinerary, sights, and ferries. I wanted her to plan with me. I couldn't get her input regarding what she wanted in the trip. She didn't know. She was happy figuring things out as we went. It was creating tension.

Then I remembered Interests.
Our Interests:
I knew that I just wanted to spend time with my brother and relax. I asked her, "What qualities or experiences are most important for you on this trip?" She had an answer for that question: She wanted to eat good food and see cultural sights.

This was too simple. I initially felt stressed again. Then I realized that the solution actually was just...simple. I could plan to my heart's content as long as she got to indulge her inner foodie and see cultural sights. There was no actual conflict.

Here's how this looks:

Table 3.2 Case Study: Vacation Planning

Issue		
How do we take a trip that we both enjoy?		
My Position		**Marta's Position**
I wanted a plan. A plan allows me to relax and enjoy the trip.		Marta didn't want me to be stressed out and ruin the trip. She also didn't want to be involved in planning.
My Interests	**Our Shared Interests**	**Marta's Interests**
• Time with my brother • Relax someplace warm • A plan, in advance, lets me feel like I wasn't working while on vacation	• Desire to relax • Desire to enjoy each other	• Eat good food • See cultural sights
Options for solution		
I could create a plan that suited my desires, without requiring her involvement, as long as we regularly had cultural and foodie experiences.		

In conflict, certain questions often come to mind: "Why is this such a big deal to him?" or, "Why is she so hung up on that solution?" or, "What are we talking about anyway?"

It is often because we are talking at the level of issues and positions and haven't delved into the deeper questions of interests.

Often enough, resolution really is that simple.

Case Study: Alaska Arctic Policy

I live in Alaska. Alaska extends into the Arctic. As a state, we are what make the United States an Arctic Nation. However, if we are lucky enough to make it onto people's maps, we're usually stuck in a box down off the Gulf of Mexico somewhere. U.S. policy makers rarely remember us. If they do, they often view us from simplistic and stereotyped perspectives.

We are politically unique. We aren't contiguous with other states. Our only neighbors are other nations—not states. We face international issues not interstate issues. We are the only non-nation region that is involved in Arctic issues. But we don't have the same negotiating power as Russia, Canada, Norway, Sweden, and so on.

The Alaska State Legislature realized that Arctic-related policies made in Washington rarely reflected the interests of Alaska. However, Alaska didn't have a coherent, unified policy platform from which to lobby.

The Legislature formed a commission to recommend this policy. The commission was formed of very diverse group of Republican and Democrat legislators as well as representatives from the military, Alaska Native groups, environmental groups, oil and gas industries, mining, fishing, and so on. Not a group of people who normally spend their free time with each other. Definitely a group that experienced some palpable preexisting conflict and distrust.

There was a strong disbelief that an effective conversation was possible. So much so, that there was hesitation on the part of some to even engage.

I guided the group through a very structured process where we:

- Clearly identified and framed the key policy issues to be addressed
- Quickly identified the initial positions of everyone in the room and then
- Pushed below to explore what made those issues important to them. That is...their interests.

Once the varied interests of the group were identified, I pulled those out and posted them on flip charts in front of the room. A shift began to take place in the group. There was a realization that there was a significant amount of agreement and overlap among underlying interests. Everyone was concerned about a healthy and fair economy. Everyone was attracted to and valued the natural beauty and environment Alaska offers. Everyone was concerned about national security.

From the common starting point of shared interests, we began to explore solutions that honored all (or as many) of the interests as possible.

It was interesting to watch traditional adversaries experience a conversation where they began to see it might be possible to work together. A very cautious optimism began to emerge. Joint statements were developed.

Roughly 90 percent of Alaska's current Arctic policy was drafted in that single six-hour session. One of the party leadership spoke with me privately afterward saying, "I didn't think it would be possible to work with (the other party.) I can't believe we were able to do this!"

The Personal Side of Interests

I'm going to make a useful generalization. As mentioned earlier, all interests probably boil down to some level of our feeling secure, significant, and/or satisfied. (Perhaps you'll find an exception and that is entirely OK.) To the degree that I'm afraid that your intent threatens my ability to attain or retain any one of these is the degree to which I feel like there is a conflict.

Often, the positions we develop unnecessarily threaten someone else's sense of security, significance, or satisfaction. We'll begin to entrench on the positions. Argue our arguments. And assume that, at the core, the other side is intentionally attacking *us*. That the desire to attack, or take, or withhold is the driving motivation of others. We can't believe the injustice or ignorance or lack of respect shown. Conflict then becomes highly personal.

We can often sidestep this by learning to clarify our own interests *while* also exploring and learning to honor the interests of others.

We tend to assume that, in disagreement, the intent of others is malicious. I've learned that, in fact, *most of the time* there is more agreement than disagreement when it comes to underlying interests.

Exploring interests is what allows you to see the entire iceberg. Knowing what is actually beneath the surface is what allows you to navigate conversations and agreements with confidence.

CHAPTER 4

Being the Change We Seek: Addressing Our Personal Approach to Conflict

Our Workplaces Are Our Mirror—Do You Like What You See?

"Be the change that you seek."

This quote is falsely attributed to Mahatma Gandhi. What he actually said invites a deeper reflection:

> We but mirror the world. All the tendencies present in the outer world are to be found in the world of our body. If we could change ourselves, the tendencies in the world would also change. As a man changes his own nature, so does the attitude of the world change toward him. This is the divine mystery supreme. A wonderful thing it is and the source of our happiness. We need not wait to see what others do.

For leaders, when it comes to conflict resolution, Gandhi's words function as an axiom. We set the tone. We give or remove permission for open communication. We avoid, defend, attack, or move to reconcile. Our workplaces reflect us.

So, our work begins with us.

As a consultant, I'm frequently asked to come and provide a team training. I always explore what prompted the request. Usually, there are descriptions of personality conflicts. Perhaps a story emerges of one or two difficult employees. In many cases, the stories reach back years.

When I began consulting, I did the off-site team trainings. I provided the HR song and dance of personality profiles and exercises. I quickly discovered that they achieve very little other than to allow management to document, "We tried."

As I developed more experience, I'd help my clients understand that I actually needed to work the dispute out with the entire team. I'd bring my entire arsenal of team assessments, personality assessments, workshops, retreats, and coaching. In a process that took many months, I would wear the team down into submission.

However, I did achieve results. Through herculean effort.

Later, with much more experience, I discovered something. This discovery allowed me to quickly achieve significant results with minimal effort.

What I discovered was that in *every instance* where a workplace has experienced a specific, long-running conflict or a tendency toward unhealthy conflicts, there was a common trait. That trait is the presence of leadership who tolerated a toxic status quo.

There are no exceptions.

I discovered something else: Leaders often prefer to view difficult situations as a *team problem* not a *leadership problem*. It takes significant humility and honesty to accept ownership of a culture and pattern of behaviors that leadership has either created or tolerated.

There are many reasons why a leader or leadership team tolerates toxic status quo. This might be fear of conflict, ego, perhaps a conflict of interest inhibits intervention, a lack of attention, or a perceived benefit gained from something in the dynamic. However, I found that in most occasions, I could turn around an entire team just by working with the leadership of the team. This takes far less effort for the team and myself.

So, I began to target working with the leaders. They are the lever that is long enough to move the world. Or at least their teams.

Honestly, though, this approach does often take significant effort for the leader. At least for a short time. I don't try to sugarcoat it. By effort, I don't mean time or cost. Both are usually lower. I mean the leader's personal willingness and vulnerability to do the work Gandhi suggests. To not wait for others and to change oneself.

The exciting thing about this work is the leaders emerge with a new level of calm confidence, self-respect, and quality relationships within their teams. They also get the significant side benefits of increases in productivity and decreases in turnover.

If I didn't see their effort they put into the process, I'd say it was magical. But I do see their efforts. They stopped avoiding and reacting and started doing the harder and vastly more rewarding work of leading.

Change begins with the leader. Change begins with you.

Typical Response to Conflict

Ken Sande, in his book *The Peacemaker (Sande 2004),* describes a range of typical responses to conflict. Below is an adapted version of his model. (Table 4.1.) In most cases we react out of either *Freeze, Flight,* or *Fight* responses. Which response we choose is often determined by whether we feel like we're in control or have power. Additionally, it is very common to begin on one side of the scale and then as the issues progress to flip to the other. For example, a supervisor may avoid addressing a consistently late employee until finally she can't take it anymore and then explodes out of anger. In another example, a business owner becomes angry at a perceived slight from a partner, retaliates through offensive comments, and overreacts in punitive decisions. Then shuts down and won't acknowledge or talk about the issue.

Table 4.1 Conflict responses

Freeze/flight reactions			Healthy resolution responses					Fight reactions		
Self-Sabotage	Denial	Avoidance	Overlook	Reconciliation	Healthy Confrontation	Mediation	Accountability	Offend	Damage	Destroy

Freeze/Flight Reactions

- **Self-Sabotage:** At its very worst, people who avoid conflict may actually sabotage themselves or their careers to avoid facing an issue. A common example of this is the scenario where an employee decides they want to quit their job and work someplace else. Changing jobs is normal. But many individuals perceive giving notice as a significant conflict. Instead of just giving notice, there can be a tendency to create a conflict that justifies ending a professional relationship. On the more extreme example, some people take such an all-or-nothing approach, that if they don't believe they can achieve their desires, they implode.

- **Denial:** Some people deny the existence of a conflict. This is often due to beliefs that conflict, any conflict, is somehow a sign of personal, professional, or moral failure. Essentially, conflict is wrong. So even in the case of healthy or appropriate disagreements there may be a minimization or denial of reality.

- **Avoidance:** The uncomfortable emotions of conflict, or perception of a negative outcome, lead us to choose to avoid addressing the issue. The illusion is that conflict can be resolved by sweeping issues under the rug. This ignores that judgments and resentments remain. The next time there is a similar offense (sometimes not even conducted by the same person) all those judgments and resentments can rise to the surface.

Fight Reactions

- **Offend:** In the face of a conflict, real or perceived, many people will react with a quick judgment and then an offensive comment, gesture, or action. This is often an attempt to retain power. It is also an attempt to cause hurt.

- **Damage:** In some conflicts, people go beyond just wanting to tweak or offend someone. They actively seek to damage the other individuals' success, credibility, or sense of worth. They may even seek to cause physical harm.

- **Destroy:** In the most extreme cases, people react to destroy another personally, professionally and, in some cases, physically.

Healthy Resolution Responses

The first thing to notice is that there are a range of healthy, appropriate options to choose from.

- **Overlook:** Some situations, offenses, and slights are best dealt with by just overlooking and forgetting them. Not every issue needs to be addressed. Not every bad driver on the road needs to be confronted. Not every bad attitude at work needs a conversation. Sometimes, it is the right response to be the Bigger Person in the situation. The challenge with this option is that it can be easy to slip from Acceptance to Avoidance. The difference, primarily, is whether: (a) anyone is being harmed or harassed by the behavior, and (b) you still carry resentment or other negative emotions over the issue.

  As leaders, if someone is being harmed or harassed it is our job to address the issue and create a safe working environment. We should never overlook the welfare of those we lead.

  If you are not able to fully let an issue go, then you are avoiding it, *not* overlooking it. If you find that you cannot overlook it, that's fine. Acknowledge it and explore ways to talk to address and resolve the issue.

- **Resolution:** Sometimes an issue cannot be overlooked and you need to approach the other person. As mentioned previously, conflicts or misunderstandings may emerge from inaccurate or incomplete information, assumptions, problematic processes, conflicting values, and so on. Having a conversation with someone, with the intent of exploring underlying shared interests, is part of building strong relationships. Additionally, there are times when we own part of the situation and need to acknowledge this as part of the resolution or reconciliation process.

- **Healthy Confrontation:** At times, it is entirely appropriate to confront poor behavior. It helps to do this in a way that focuses on the *behavior* and not on the person. It is most effective when done in a way that affirms the other person and the relationship, if possible, but address the problematic behavior and desired change.

- **Mediation:** Sometimes conversations are either so complicated or emotional that we just need help. Seeking someone to either simply sit in as a witness to our conversation can be helpful for some people. Sometimes it helps to have someone facilitate the conversation. This is called mediation. Mediation is a very high success rate process. Most skilled mediators experience between 80 and 95 percent success in helping people achieve resolution.

- **Accountability:** An often misunderstood option by some people is when others need to be held to account. This usually looks like making a report to some kind of authority. This could be management calling a professional association or regulatory body or the police. It could include filing a claim in court. This response is appropriate when dealing in a scenario where someone is unwilling or unresponsive to other approaches to conflict resolution. It is often the solution when someone is engaging in unethical or dangerous behavior. Care needs to be exercised because some people abuse options for accountability. For example, a significant number of the cases in the court system are the result of one or more people avoiding dealing with an issue directly. In my experience, many (not all) litigated cases start out as problems that were avoided or denied by at least one party until the other filed a suit. At this point, the conversation shifts to fight mode.

Being the Change We Seek: Addressing Our Personal Approach to Conflict

I practice Brazilian Jiu-Jitsu. (I can only handle so much empathy and understanding. Then I just need to wrassle.) In every class, we spend time drilling specific moves. These are practiced in ideal scenarios, with a willing and helpful partner. We get to practice choking, sweeping, throwing, submitting someone—again and again. Instructors wander around and coach us. It doesn't always seem easy but it does seem doable.

Then we spend time grappling. This is 100 percent, all-out, going for it. When I was new, everything I just learned turned to mud. Our previously willing and helpful partner is now doing his or her best to choke me out or force me to submit. I couldn't use what I had learned. The move didn't seem to work.

It is very easy to develop tunnel vision, to get claustrophobic when someone is laying across your head. It's easy to react, hyperventilate, and forget every lesson that was just learned.

I very quickly discovered that Jiu-Jitsu is largely a mental game. When the overwhelming crush happens, can I keep my head? Or do I start freak out? Before I can ever have the faintest hope of consistently being able to control where a match goes, I need to control where my own emotions and mind go.

Conflict is an incredibly emotional and triggering experience for many people. This is true even if the triggers result in someone shutting down emotionally and *not* consciously feeling the conflict. As a result, it often doesn't matter what I cognitively know about conflict, negotiating, listening, personalities or anything else if, when conflict occurs, I spike to a *Freeze/Flight* or *Fight* reaction.

Since I will face conflicts for the whole, entire rest of my life, it makes the most sense (and is the only practical reality) that I first begin with changing me. That's where I have the most control and influence. There are three aspects of personal change that will allow me to respond more effectively in conflict. First, how I see myself; second, how I see others, and last, how I see the world and everything else.

Facing Ourselves: How I See Myself

How we see ourselves, or our *Self-Image* is developed over many thousands of encounters in our life. Particularly our early life. As children, we learn about who we are by the image of ourselves reflected back to us by our parents, family, teachers, friends, and others.

There are two primary categories of messages that we are shaped by:

1. **The Message of Self-Efficacy:** Self-efficacy is the belief that I can and do influence my world. Most children start out assuming they

influence their worlds. At least my kids did. As children, we all grow up learning lessons about what we can and cannot control or influence. As the father of three, parenting sometimes feels largely like trying to regain my own self-efficacy from the tyranny of toddlers.

As a leader, the greater my sense of self-efficacy is, the more likely I'll be able to believe that I can act to create resolution. The more able I will be to recognize my own strengths and failings. The more I will be able to choose to grow.

The opposite is also true. The weaker my sense of self-efficacy is, the more likely I will act passively, or react to get vengeance, to avoid, deny, or shift blame and to not believe that my growth is either an option or relevant.

2. **The Message of Self-Esteem:** Self-Esteem is the belief that I have value and I can bring value to others. It has nothing to do with me liking or accepting everything about myself.

   I become resilient when, in the face of criticism or conflict, I remain confident in my own value and my ability to bring value. This doesn't mean I don't make mistakes, fail others, or act badly and need to own it. This means that I see those actions as behaviors that I can change. Not definers of who I am.

   Someone with weak self-esteem will find that their personal sense of value or ability to bring value is easily threatened. This might be the frontline, entry-level employee who doesn't quite have the confidence to speak up loud enough for the customer to hear. This might be the CEO who is easily bent out of shape at the slightest hint of criticism.

   In conflict, someone with weak self-esteem will either quickly acquiesce to others as a way of avoiding conflict. Or they will have strong overreactions (defensive and offensive) designed to protect themselves from slights, criticisms, and attacks—many of which are imagined.

Why It Matters

My ability to interpret reality, make choices, and respond to others is bounded by my ability to access and recognize accurate information. Some people call this "bounded rationality." We all only know and see in part. Since I am the only constant character in the story of my life, the way I interpret the reality of myself, my choices, and responses are highly impacted by how I see myself.

Despite this, self-image is one of those topics that most people don't spend time reflecting on. But when you ask them to, it often generates strong reactions. One common reaction is to be strongly dismissive, "I don't buy into that self-image stuff. Who cares how you feel, just get out there and do the right thing." Another common reaction tends to be *victim stance.* To immediately start thinking about all the hurts and disappointments experienced. Past and often distant experiences are blamed for current decisions and reactions.

Many disputes are prolonged or escalated, due to issues outside of the actual dispute. Often, one or more parties to the dispute are in some sense fighting (or hiding) for their lives. They believe *they* are at stake. Not just the issue the conflict seems to be about. People with poor self-image tend to see issues in conflict as a proxy for the questions of, "Am I valued?" or "Do I have power?"

When a leader hasn't resolved these questions for themselves, they will persistently require that others answer those questions for them. This can be expected to create relationship problems. It will definitely create workplace problems.

For example: A conversation about the budget is about balancing the numbers for one person. But for someone else, who isn't resolved in their sense of *self-efficacy,* they may compulsively need to act to prove they have power. So, they might often appear to be contradictory or unwilling to compromise. While the issues are important to the person, staying *powerful* may be more important.

It is one reason why conflict can feel so emotionally intense and confusing.

Signs of Poor Self-Image in Leaders

Below are lists of behaviors that may indicate that a leader has a poor self-image. A caution as you read through this list. It isn't designed to enable you to label or diagnose someone else. It is designed as a tool to spur self-reflection.

Aggressive Behaviors

- Controlling decisions
- Perfectionistic/critical
- Bossy
- Bullying
- Revenge/spiteful
- Gossip

Passive-Defensive Behaviors

- Avoidance
- Seeking approval
- Isolation
- Acquiescence
- Revenge
- Gossip
- Controlling information
- Controlling access to others or opportunities

Other Signs of Poor Self-Image in Leaders

- Frequently feeling down or depressed
- Frequently angry
- Low energy
- Lack of drive or motivation
- Feeling helplessness
- Absenteeism
- Illness
- Substance abuse or other compulsive behaviors

As a leadership coach, I do watch for these behaviors in the clients I work with. I've not found it to be productive to tell someone, "'I think what is going on here is that your self-image is poor." Instead, I use the information to help develop a strategy for serving them more effectively.

It provides insight into *possible* drivers behind how that leader might receive and interpret information. It helps me ask better questions around their choices and behaviors. I'm not a therapist. I don't dig into their childhood stories (although, those stories would often shed light on current dynamics). But if I believe that a leader's poor self-image is part of the dynamics of a conflict, I realize that I can't just address the conflict itself. This person's responses are fueled by something that preexisted the conflict.

What Can I Do About My Self-Image?

The most common reaction, when I present the information above, is for people to start reflecting back stories about business partners, past employers, spouses, or parents. It is helpful to recognize these things. But you can't do much, or anything, about those other people. You can do a whole lot about yourself. Below is a list of questions to start your process of growth:

- How easily or often do I feel disrespected by others? Ignored? Disregarded?
- In my last three interpersonal business interactions (team meetings, one-on-one conversations, project conversations, and so on) how strongly was I oriented toward bringing value to the others involved? How strongly was I oriented to getting value out of those interactions?
- How much time or emotional energy do I spend on what I can actually do something about? How does that compare with the time I give to topics I can't do anything about?

Six Steps for Developing a Strong Self-Image

Step One: Change Your Mirrors

No man is an island...

—John Dunne

You are the average of your five closest friends.

—Jim Rohn

I'm a pretty independent guy. I'm comfortable doing things my own way. It can be difficult to accept how much I'm influenced by those who surround me.

Changing our mirrors is challenging. It is also the choice that will have the greatest impact. The mirrors I'm referring to are the relationships closest to you.

We know that children need social interaction to develop both physically and mentally. In fact, they will suffer interrupted development and health problems without nurturing relationships. This is true even if their physical needs are met. It's within those early relationships that we, as children first learned to *see* who we are. We learn who we are through the image reflected back to us by others.

Unfortunately, not every image reflected back to us was caring, accurate, nurturing, or helpful. As a result, as children, we may have developed a confused or negative or just inaccurate picture of who we are, our value, and the value we offer others.

For good or for bad, I can't do anything about the people I spent time with as a child. I can't do anything about the messages I received many years ago. Neither can you.

However, as an adult I can choose. I need to choose.

Years ago, I realized I was stuck. I felt stuck relationally, professionally, and spiritually. In a moment of awareness, I looked around at who I spent time with. I noticed that most of the people whom I spent the most time with were stuck as well. They weren't happy professionally, but they weren't trying to change anything. They weren't happy in their marriages or family lives, but they didn't seem to be trying to build anything. They just weren't happy. But they weren't acting to create change.

I didn't fully understand this self-image principle at the time; but, I knew I wanted to surround myself with people who were growing. Specifically, I desired to spend my time with people who enjoyed their marriages, were thriving professionally, and were flourishing spiritually.

Professionally, I started hiring coaches (yes, you can and should pay for some of these relationships). I started traveling, regularly, to spend time with a community of consultants who were at the top of their game. I started spending more time with friends who were happy in their marriages and families. The kinds of people who actively invested in building their closest relationships. I started working with someone on my spiritual development. I joined a community of people who supported each other's spiritual growth. I became intentional about whom I chose to spend my time with. I prioritized time with people who reflected attributes I wanted in my life.

This was *not* easy. It was not without cost.

Yet, at no point have I regretted it. When I first made this hard shift in relationships, it coincided, not uncoincidentally, with my getting married, a transformation in my business model, and breaking out of the spiritual doldrums. I've experienced sustained and sometimes dramatic growth because of *who* I surround myself with.

Ready to break out? Start by asking yourself these questions:

- Who are your five or six closest friends? Are you content with the average this creates in you?
- Are you attracted to healthy people? Why or why not?
- Name one to two people who exhibit qualities you'd like to grow in that you can begin building relationships with. What will be your next step?

Don't skip Step One if you truly want to change your self-image. The remaining steps are all much easier.

Step Two: Three Gratitudes

Gratitude is one of the most powerful attitudes and perspectives that someone can cultivate. It combines both humility and the ability to appreciate or to see good. The humility is necessary to be able to receive, graciously, from others. The ability to appreciate is important because, as to paraphrase Zig Ziglar, "Anybody can be a *fault* finder. I want to be a *good* finder."

Begin each day with a list of three things that you are grateful for. I encourage you to think of new things you are grateful for each day, and I encourage you to write them down. It helps make them more real to you. As you do this, your perspective will begin to change. For twenty-one days, begin each morning by writing a list of three things that you are grateful for.

Step Three: Plan and Reflect on Priorities

To address the beliefs that I can offer value and that my actions have impact requires that I act. Here are two small actions which make a big difference:

- **Plan Your Priority:** Each day identify only one or two accomplishments that you will pursue. You can make your to-do list as large as you like. But choose only one or two priorities. This is your focus for the day. I plan for one personal and one professional priority. When you've accomplished it, you can identify a new priority for the remainder of the day. That's how you work through a list. As compared to multi-tasking, this is a far more efficient and effective approach for increasing your ability to accomplish your goals.
- **Reflect on Yesterday's Priority:** Each day, reflect on what you actually did. You'll likely see that you are following through on your planned impact. However, if you didn't do what you planned, still find one or two successes that happened. If you are like many people, it's too easy to look at your day and fixate on the distance left remaining in the journey not on the progress made. As you make this a daily practice, you'll start to develop a robust inventory of ways that you've acted and made a difference. It will shift your perspective and help you see your impact.

Step Four: Offer Value to Others

Very similar to Step Three, think of one way that you can bring value to the life of someone else. What is one way that you can serve, communicate appreciation, or improve someone's condition?

- **Plan Your Impact:** Each day identify one new way you will bring value to someone else today. Simply choosing to express a specific appreciation or gratitude is enough for this exercise. But you can also choose to serve someone, be generous to someone, or bring value in any other way.

- **Review Your Impact:** Each day, reflect back on what you actually did yesterday. How did you communicate appreciation? How did you serve? How did you bring value? What seemed to be appreciated? Keep a list. An inventory. If you keep doing this for a year, you'll start to see hundreds of ways you bring value to others.

Step Five: Listen to/Read Encouraging Biographies, Podcasts, and so on

So much of today's media is negative and critical. Regardless of political persuasion, there is a strong tendency to take on and champion a victim mentality (e.g., us versus them). This habit is mentally and attitudinally toxic. Instead, immerse yourself in the stories of people who've overcome challenges and made significant accomplishments. This is a powerful way to shape the messaging that we surround ourselves with. It shapes our perspective of what's possible and gives us insights into how it's possible.

- What inspirational figure could you read about this month? What do you hope to learn from their story?
- Whose positive message can you listen to this week on podcasts or your preferred medium? What do you hope to learn from them?
- What should I "detox" from? What should I stop reading or listening to?

Step Six: Focused Skill Development

Building your skills definitely helps. As I coach people through challenging processes, I've often observed an almost visible difference in someone's self-image as they grow in whatever skill(s) they are working on. Pick one specific skill to grow in, block out time and work on it until you've achieved competency. (For most skills, competency is more valuable than mastery.) This could be as simple as learning to quickly prioritize (Step Three), or joining Toastmasters, or taking cooking classes. It's up to you; but the process of intentionally growing and achieving a new skill set will help shape your positive self-image.

- What is one skill that I can begin to block out time to master?
- What is the next step that I need to take to make sure this happens?

21 Day Experiment

Make an experiment out of the steps above. Commit to doing as many of them as possible for twenty-one days. Twenty-one days is enough time for most people to start to recognizably begin to feel differently. I've given this or similar exercises to clients and they've all reported a positive impact.

Interestingly enough, this kind of approach is really about lifestyle and mindset change. It's not something you can do and then it's done. Similar to diet, sleep or fitness – it's a form of emotional fitness. It's something that needs to be maintained. But, as in most fitness decisions, small commitments are a good place to start.

Try out the steps above for the next twenty-one days. It'll cost you nothing and may start to change everything.

Self-Image Transformation

As you can see, transforming how you see yourself is within your grasp. While therapy may be a part of this process and might be very helpful, in most cases it isn't necessary. Just making very small but intentional steps, consistently, will result in personal change. Faster than you'd imagine.

As a leader, the stronger and healthier your self-image is, the fewer toxic conflicts you'll find yourself in. You'll be triggered less easily. You'll be able to confront poor behavior more confidently and without personalizing it. Not only will you be more effective in conflict, you'll also be a far more effective leader.

When I Look at You: How I See Others

As happens in the hallowed halls of Harvard, two sets of students were given two different groups of rats to run through a maze. Dr. Rosenthal, who was running the experiment, informed the students that one set of the rats were bright—smart and good at running mazes. The other set of rats dull—slow and easily confused in a maze (Rosenthal and Fode 1963).

He asked them to run their rats and score their times. As expected, the bright rats performed brilliantly and quickly made it to the end of the maze. The dull rats struggled in the same maze. Uncertain, lost, or confused—they just had a more difficult time quickly navigating it. Or so the students thought.

There were, in fact, no bright or dull rats. All the rats were normal lab rats. Dr. Rosenthal had randomly assigned each rat to a group labeled bright or dull. Subconsciously, this difference in expectations led the students to relate to the rats differently. The normal lab rats performed up or down to the student's expectations.

If this is true for rats, can this also happen in our workplace relationships? If we expect someone to be annoying or confrontational or rude, do we somehow create self-fulfilling prophecies?

This study has actually been repeated many times. In fact, it is now called the expectancy effect. Many of these studies explore how the expectations of teachers impact the performance of students (Rosenthal and Jacobson 1963). The results are the same as with the rats. Teachers were introduced to students at the beginning of the year. The students were, unknown to them, randomly labeled in some tests as High or Low Performing or, in other tests, "Expected/not expected to bloom this year." Time and again, students prove to live up to the unspoken expectations.

"I Love You. Now Brace Yourself."

Leadership is a relationship. As leaders, we build the cultures we are surrounded by. We often have a higher amount of control, even, over whom we are surrounded by.

However, we rarely consider that *how* we see and relate to others influences the nature and frequency of disagreements that will occur.

I was in a meeting with one of my fastest growing clients. In the meeting was the owner of the company and his emerging senior leadership team. I was helping them have a conversation around some difficult topics. The staff were frustrated with some of the owner's current choices.

The woman who (shortly after) became the CEO of his company, who had been quiet for a time, finally spoke up, "I love you. Now brace yourself." Then she laid out how the owner's actions were in violation of his own stated standards and frustrating the company's growth.

The owner blinked, sat back, and listened. At first, he made a couple of half-hearted defensive statements. Then he stopped.

"No, you're right." He said, "I need to go back and fix those things." What this meant, and everyone in the room knew it, was that the next year of his life would be dedicated to correcting some earlier mistakes. This would significantly limit some of his future choices and options. But ultimately, it would allow the company to grow and eventually allow him some of the freedom he had prematurely pursued.

This particular owner is not a pushover. But I have observed him, over the years, as he has shaped a culture that allows his staff to directly confront him when they believe he is wrong.

For him to do this, he needs to have a strong enough self-image to not feel threatened. But he also needs to have a relationship with his staff, where he sees them as people whom he respects. He needs to see them as people who have something valuable to offer.

What happens is they grow up into this picture.

This changes the nature of their conflicts. I've watched his teams have very loud, very vocal arguments over issues. I've watched new members of the team, who were unused to this, physically recoil and try to move away from the conversation. At times, it can be that intense.

However, what quickly becomes clear is that the owner deeply respects his employees. He takes time to understand their concerns. He isn't shaken by whether they know how to appropriately express their concerns to him.

He doesn't allow their emotion to create a personal issue.

This wouldn't be possible if he didn't choose to trust them, to trust their intent.

I'm not saying that you can work with anyone, be nice, and they'll live to your expectations. Some people consistently make foolish, ill-informed choices. Some people are driven by malicious intent.

However, most people aren't. Most people want to work well together.

Projection and Transference

These are terms that tend to show up more often in a counselor's office. But they are just as common on the worksite or in the board room.

Projection: Projection occurs when I make the mistake of putting myself in someone's shoes and assuming the way they fit on me is the way they fit on them.

Or, more directly, I assume that what I feel about something is what other people feel about it.

For example, if I tend to resent other people's success, I might assume that other people resent my own.

The truth might be that the other people don't care, aren't paying attention anyways, or even that they admire my success.

However, since I attribute to others a feeling or response that isn't really theirs, I may overreact to them. I might read into someone's comments. I may overpersonalize a critique or suggestion. I may begin to act in ways that are confusing to the other. As a result, I start to generate conflict.

Another example might be if an employee is struggling in a particular area. We might remember how we felt embarrassed when we struggled in that same area. Now, as a leader instead of bringing in appropriate correction or help, we want to avoid embarrassing our employee, so we avoid addressing the issue.

The issue doesn't get addressed. Then it gets repeated. We keep avoiding it until it finally reaches a point of extremity where it can't be ignored. Then we might blow up and overreact. Conflict.

Transference: Transference occurs when I take the emotions that I experienced with either someone else, or the same person at another point in time and experience those emotions, now, in the current context.

For example, perhaps a colleague reminds me of a past business partner. A partner with whom I had a significant falling out. Their mannerisms are similar, their approach to issues is similar. They even kind of dress the same. I may start to transfer the distrust, guardedness, or resentment that I felt toward my former partner onto this new colleague. Conflict.

Something many of my coaching clients struggle with is experiencing past-self transference from their employees or colleagues. Let's say I'm working with an executive who was known for being sharp and abrasive. We might work together for six months and her behaviors change dramatically.

Then, during a meeting where there are some hot topics to be discussed, she finds that while she's taking the time to listen and be more diplomatic, she's still being related to with kid gloves. When she explores this, she's told that, "We don't want you to bite off our heads again."

It's for this reason, in my executive coaching, I often work with my clients to target change in both their behavior and the perception of their behavior.

We Create Our Realities

Either way, you can see that how we view other people are sometimes mistaken. If we tend to mistakenly view people from a negative perspective, we create situations where they may live *down* to our expectations.

How we see people is strongly connected to how we see ourselves. It also shapes the nature and frequency of the conflicts we experience.

How I Read the News: How I See the World and Everything Else

In South Sudan, the cyclical experience is of famine, war, and multiple outbreaks of disease. The kinds of diseases that have been wiped out nearly everywhere else on earth.

In 2003, to prepare to go in, the UN required that we be shuttled through a series of briefings and trainings. I learned about the war, about the politics, about how to relate with the military, rebels, and tribal factions. I learned about how to survive aerial bombings (get low and pray), how to avoid setting off land mines (don't go anywhere), and how to escape a helicopter attack (you won't).

We learned about land navigation and survival. Or enough to give us a false sense of confidence. We learned about how to filter our water and learned about all the little bugs waiting to become big bugs inside of us if we didn't.

We learned that Sudan was a place of tremendous need, scarcity, and deprivation. As a result, we traveled as a self-contained unit, packing up and flying in all the food, fuel, tools, and gear that we would need. We established high security protocols and precautions. I was excited but apprehensive. Nearly everything and anything I learned about was associated with a threat.

Once I was in Sudan, I had an experience that radically shook that perspective. It was a simple experience. It has never left me.

I was talking with a local leader one day. We were standing near a trail by his tukul, or mud hut. Another man walked up. He said he was traveling through to a larger community several days' walk away. He was nearly naked and carried a spear over his shoulder. At the end of his spear he had a small bundle in a handkerchief. Like a hobo.

That was it. We said our pleasantries and he was off down the trail.

I realized something. When I looked down that trail I saw danger, disease, and famine. I saw that I needed to be on the defensive.

When he looked down that trail he assumed he'd find food, safe places to sleep, and a successful journey to do his business. He saw opportunity.

The way we view our worlds has a lot to do with our experiences. I didn't know the gentlemen. But I think it's fair to assume that his upbringing was more challenging than my own. So, while experiences matter, how we view our present and future matters more.

If I view the world as a place that is out to get me, a place where the economy is always perilous, where cynicism is the only right attitude toward leadership, where the labor pool these days can't be trusted, where mistakes or oversights are always intentional offenses—I'm not prone to be particularly creative or effective at problem solving when conflict occurs. I'll primarily be oriented toward protecting myself and distrusting the motivations and intent of others.

However, if I view the world as a place of opportunity, where problems are routinely solved, better solutions are creatively found, where there are many people working selflessly on behalf of others—I'm more prone to believe that conflict is an experience that can be worked through. Not only that, but there can be deeper and more meaningful understanding, trust, and collaboration on the other side of conflict.

The information that I expose myself to, the experiences that I create for myself, the relationships I spend time with, all add up to shaping my larger perspective. As children, we are limited in our options. As adults, we need to increasingly learn to own and choose those options.

You may, rightfully, be saying, "But not everyone can be trusted! It *is* a dog-eat-dog world out there!" That's true. It can be. We should walk with that awareness.

But that isn't the entire truth. There can be much more to our potential experience than just trying to survive. For that to happen, we have to be able to see it. To be able to see it, we need to allow that kind of information to fill our field of vision.

I've learned, in real life, that it is entirely possible to enjoy a relaxing Saturday picnic next to a minefield. If I focused on the mines, it created stress. Not only that but it tended to become the focus of my attention. (I was 19 the first time I had this experience. At that point it was dangerous to focus my attention on a mine field. I ended up throwing rocks into it to see what would happen. Fortunately, I never hit one.)

As it turns out, land mines—as dangerous as they genuinely are—don't jump up and chase you around. If, while picnicking, I focused on the sunshine, the clouds, the spring air, the smell of the earth, the sound of the trees, and enjoying the people I was with—it was an entirely different experience. I wasn't losing perspective on reality. I was just choosing which perspective that I allowed to be the dominant flavor of reality.

That choice is what opens or closes the doors to many other choices.

CHAPTER 5

The Four Steps to Resolution: It Really Is This Simple

In Brazilian Jiu-Jitsu, we have a helpful perspective of *high percentage moves* and *low percentage moves*. It's another way of saying this defense or attack will be more likely to be successful or less likely. It helps me move from more black and white thinking of "this works" or "this doesn't work."

Additionally, it allows for a perspective that a move doesn't need to work entirely. I may not completely escape from someone. I may not complete a submission. It can be sufficient if it just improves my position. In fact, the more experienced someone is, the more prepared they are to make a chain of attempts until they complete their goal.

Similarly, there are no magic codes or sequences in leadership. There is nothing that will always, definitely work in organizational relationships. There is nothing that will predictably resolve all conflict.

What we endeavor to do is learn to:

- Increase the likelihood of a sustainable resolution when conflict occurs.
- Decrease the likelihood of unhealthy conflict occurring.
- Increase our ability to shift from one tool or approach to another.

If you only focus on trying to avoid conflict, you inevitably create it by not addressing issues that needed to be addressed early on. If you don't try to mitigate the frequency or intensity of conflict and only try to resolve it once it occurs, you create a high-stress environment that wastes time and energy by confusing drama with productivity.

The effective leader will progressively learn to decrease unhealthy and unproductive approaches and increase effective and healthy approaches.

Additionally, it helps to recognize and accept an improved situation. This may be where full resolution has not been achieved, full agreement not arrived at, or full trust not restored but any of which is improved. It helps to recognize this gives us a different and more advantageous position from which we can continue to work on the relationship. Not all conflicts need to resolve entirely at once.

Just don't confuse a partially resolved conflict with an entirely resolved one.

I want to introduce you to a high percentage approach to resolving interpersonal conflict. It will work or at least improve your situation the majority of the time. I call this High Percentage approach: The Four Steps to Resolution. If you thoughtfully work through each of these steps, you will significantly increase your chances of entirely resolving your conflict. Even if you fall short of full resolution, your situation will likely be improved.

The Four Steps to Resolution are:

Step 1: Clarify what I really want
Step 2: Accept responsibility
Step 3: Ask for what I really want
Step 4: Clarify where we go from here

Step One: Clarify What I Really Want

At the beginning of an intervention, I'll often sit down with people and ask them something like, "What does fixing this look like to you?"

Most people struggle to answer the question. This is especially true when the conflict has become highly personalized. They may say something like, "I don't want him to act like such a bully." Or "I don't want to feel so stressed when we meet."

Those are both valid desires. But neither are easy targets for someone else. They are too vague or ambiguous. What we want to do is make it as easy for the other party, and for ourselves, to know what resolution looks like.

In very substantive disputes, the statement might start as something like, "I want them to pay $500,000 to compensate me for my loss." Or "I want them to give me this position and set of responsibilities."

Even in these cases, where it seems very obvious what they want, it actually isn't. I'll often ask someone what $500,000 means to them. Or what getting that position would communicate to them.

They'll often respond with saying what they really want is an apology. Or that they want respect and acknowledgment for their contribution.

The point is we often aren't clear on what it is we want. What we believe we want is often only symbolic for an underlying desire or interest.

When this is the case, a $500,000 settlement may be accepted but both parties may still walk away feeling upset. Especially in business, there is a tendency to mistakenly believe that enough money should fix most things. Or that it is the only option available.

I've mediated litigated cases where I've watched parties entirely and voluntarily drop their claims, when the opposing party sincerely apologized. That was what they really wanted. An honest and open acknowledgment that they had been wronged. The money was just a poor proxy. If a litigant had received the money but not an acknowledgment, the resentment would likely be retained. Only a surface and possibly unsustained resolution would be achieved.

In the workplace, with ongoing relationships, a partial solution means the conflict will often reemerge. So, as much as possible, we want to try to identify the underlying interests or desires. This is where a sustainable resolution can be built.

Question 1: What does "fixing this" look like to me? What makes this solution important to me?

Now, we'll dig a little deeper. At the core, difficult-to-resolve conflicts are often stuck because one or more people feel that deeply held values have been violated. Understanding what those are helps dramatically in shaping an acceptable resolution.

If we feel like what we really want was something like "To be respected," this is a solid start. The next step is to describe what behaviors, from someone else, indicate respect to me. At this point, others can clearly understand the solution we are searching for.

Question 2: What are my three highest values that I believe should guide how people should relate to other in a situation like this?

-

-

-

Take the time to answer this question. It is easiest if you try to answer the question with single word names for values. As an example, nearly everyone will use language that describes at least one of the values of *Integrity/Honesty* or *Respect*. You may arrive at different values. That's entirely fine. Don't worry if you don't come up with three. One or two is a good starting place.

Step Two: Exploring (and Accepting) Responsibility

In Step One, we start to define, for ourselves, what a successful resolution might look like. This is valuable because it provides focus for the conversation.

In Step Two, we create the conditions within which resolution is possible. In this step, we're looking for any way that our actions or attitudes may have contributed to the conflict. It begins with an honest examination of the question, "Do I own any of this?"

Years ago, I came home after work. My wife was already home. Upon entering our home, I made a flippant comment. Sometime later in the evening, I noticed that my wife seemed withdrawn. Later she made a remark that I felt was rude. I asked if there was something wrong.

"No." She replied. However, there clearly was. As I tried to dig into it, she started to shut down. I kept pushing believing that I was on the "high moral ground" of the responsible spouse working through issues. Eventually though, I grew frustrated at her unwillingness to talk and some of her remarks.

This escalated into an argument which spiraled out of control. I ended up getting up and leaving, slamming the door behind me to take a drive and try to cool off.

Now, I had already begun professionally working with content similar to what I'm presenting here. As I cooled off, driving through unfamiliar neighborhoods, I couldn't figure out what her problem was. It felt as if I had done nothing wrong, at all, until I ran out of patience at her attitude. Maybe that was what I needed to acknowledge. But that would likely just inflame the situation. Finally, I decided to just ask her, "Was there something that I did?"

I came home. She was upset and barely willing to entertain more conversation. I let her know I wanted to try to find a reset button. I asked if there was something that I did—because I wasn't seeing it.

She pointed to the sarcastic comment I made when I first walked in the door. It was a throwaway remark that meant little to me. But it had impacted her. As she chewed on it, it grew inside her until we experienced open conflict.

Once I was able to own and apologize for the remark that I had made, we were able to move on and resolve the rest of the conversation.

It would be nice to think that workplace conflicts aren't as emotionally sensitive as marriage conflicts can sometimes be. But they can be. Sometimes even more so, because there is often less of a commitment to each other try to figure out how to work through it.

Step Two is the most powerful of the Four Steps. It is also, frequently, the most challenging for people. Most people I work with begin by insisting that the responsibility or fault lies entirely with the other party. While there is a chance that this may be true, I've found that with a little reflection, many people discover that they've also contributed to the conflict in some way. By completing this step, you dramatically improve the chances of a successful (and often much faster) resolution.

In my experience, roughly 90 percent of the disputes that I've mediated resolve. Nearly all of them are between parties where one or both thought resolution was impossible. What I've found is that only two conditions need to be met for resolution to be possible:

A *willingness to try* on the part of all parties. Even if one or more of the parties doesn't think trying will help. In my experience, as long as they are willing, success is actually highly likely.

A willingness to act in *Good Faith.* This just means that each party honestly comes to the conversation with an intent to be honest, act with integrity, and to follow through on whatever agreements are arrived at.

Most people want to move on to Step Three. That is where they believe they'll find resolution. However, many times, the key to resolution is in Step Two: Taking Appropriate Responsibility.

However, if you find yourself struggling with this step at this time, you might want to read and answer some of the questions on Step Three first. However, I encourage you to come back and think Step Two through before talking to the other person. Otherwise, you significantly reduce the likelihood that your efforts will be successful.

The fact is that it is very rare for a conflict to occur where both sides haven't somehow contributed to it. However, what our contribution is may not be obvious to us. I don't know anyone who likes exploring this. I still haven't arrive at a place where I enjoy this kind of reflection. But I've learned that it's critical.

The power of Step Two is that if we can make a sincere acknowledgment of our responsibility, it tends to bleed off the pressure of the situation. It is the key to gaining the attention and openness of the other party. It gives our efforts to resolve the conflict.

More importantly, if we're at some level of fault, it's the right thing to do to acknowledge it.

Step Two is difficult. At least some of the reasons most people find it to be difficult are:

1. It feels unjust. We want justice in the situation and there is a fear that if I acknowledge any ownership of the situation I'm letting the other person off the hook.
2. It requires vigorous honesty and humility. Both character traits can be difficult to express. Particularly to someone whom we don't believe has been honest or humble toward us.

3. We might not know how we've contributed. We just can't see it.

When you engage in Step Two, you are taking a leadership role in changing the dynamic of the conversation. It feels risky. It also rarely offers immediate emotional satisfaction.

So, it requires courage. What it does do is set the conversation up to be successful.

Dealing With Assumptions

In nearly every conflict that I have mediated, there has been a deficit of accurate information between the parties. It is rarely the case that both sides are working from the same information.

Many conflicts are built or exaggerated from assumptions. We assume what someone's intent was. We assume we know what someone was thinking. Our assumptions explain what is going on and provide a rationale for our reactions. We become emotionally invested in our assumptions and struggle to allow them to be examined.

What assumptions might I be making about the facts or the motives of the other person(s)? What "Facts" have I accepted as true that haven't actually been confirmed?

Here is the crux of Step Two. We tend to view conflicts through the lens of how we've been wronged or offended. While that all might be true, it may also be true that we've wronged or offended the other party as well.

In conflict, we tend to fixate on the slights or wrongs we've experienced. Real or perceived. The people we are in conflict with are doing this as well.

If we are able to reflect, listen to, and own any contribution we have made, we start to remove the fuel from the fire.

In Step One, the two most common values that people describe are Honesty and/or Respect. Yours may be different. That's fine.

But let's take Honesty. Let's say this is a core value for me. I might feel frustrated because I don't believe you have given me complete or accurate information. I might even believe that information has been distorted. So, my value of Honesty has been violated.

However, if in the course of my conversation with you, I also withhold information, don't acknowledge my responsibility or am unwilling to listen to honest feedback about how I've been experienced—I am no longer living in alignment with my own values.

The only way to feel psychologically comfortable with this internal misalignment with my own values is to refuse to hold myself to account and view the other person as being all wrong.

A way of framing this for myself, that I find helpful, is "Even if I'm only 10 percent responsible, I can own 100 percent of that 10 percent." To be willing to do that has rarely meant that I'm left holding the bag for the entire 100 percent. In nearly all cases, it has deescalated the conversation, made it feel safer, and allowed the other party to open up about how they've contributed to the conflict as well.

How does the other person(s) experience me? In what ways might I not be living up to my own values? What might fully extending my values to them look like in this situation?

There are occasions where we may not share any responsibility. I have encountered situations where it appears that there really is no shared responsibility. However, I have also found that this is rare. Rare enough to justify at least exploring the question if we've contributed in any way.

Step Three: Ask for What I Want

Step Three. The step everyone wants to get to. How to confront the other person. Or, to put it more gently, how to ask them to change or give us what we want. This is the part of the conversation many people jump into prematurely. It's also where we see the biggest escalations of conflict—if Steps One and Two haven't been completed.

A Thought Experiment

Imagine an unresolved conflict that you have recently experienced.

Let the faces of the people involved come to mind.

Identify the emotions that you feel. Give the conflict a name.

Now, imagine if the other party really prepared themselves with Step One and Step Two before they came to you.

Imagine that they opened the conversation by acknowledging of how their actions or attitudes or omissions have contributed to the conflict. They took full ownership of their responsibility *without trying to make a false peace.*

Does anything shift in you with that acknowledgment?

It is very likely that your attitude will have started to change toward them. They might appear to be somewhat more genuine or sincere. You might be more open to what they want to talk about. Even if they wanted to ask for some kind of change from you.

That's the power of the first two steps.

But the problem may not be resolved. Apologies and expressions of ownership are often only a start. Not a conclusion. You are still feeling that a wrong has been done to you. Or an issue is still out there. Avoiding or denying that doesn't resolve it. Learning to appropriately ask for what we want does support resolution.

Here are four principles for preparing for an effective conversation:

1. **Separate the problem from the person.** Focus on the specific thing, attitude, behavior, or agreement you are looking for. Don't make critical or generalized statements about their character or value. Don't make universal statements "You *always/never....*"

   These kinds of statements will be perceived as an attack on their personhood. That will usually be defended. However, if you specifically point out a behavior, "You were 20 minutes late to the meeting today." The other person may still be defensive, but not as defensive as compared to, "You are constantly late! I can never rely on you to show up on time for anything!"

2. **Focus on a single issue.** Stay tightly focused on one specific problem. Don't try to address every grievance you have. If you've allowed a

backlog of grievances to build up, I recommend choosing just one to work on. You'll often find that the dynamics of interpersonal conflict are such that if you address one issue well, other issues become easier to resolve due to the newly developed goodwill. So, for this conversation, pick one issue.

3. **Reflect on their interests.** Both your interests and theirs are at play. It is often valuable to take some time and reflect on what their interests may be. If you don't know, you can develop questions to ask them. Don't jump to conclusions about their interests. But if you think you gain insight through this exercise, it's worth exploring.

4. **Be open to the possibility of more than one acceptable solution.** Avoid ultimatums or *take it or leave it* approaches.

    Present what you have to say as if you are presenting an option. Or one idea. They may engage you and have other ideas. Or they want to modify your idea or negotiate. Some of their ideas you may not have imagined yet. Some could possibly be better than your own or better than what you hoped for.

    Template: The template below is just a guide. It is helpful. Follow it to the degree that it is helpful. There is purpose behind the structure of it though. It follows this approach:

1. *Affirmation:* This opening affirmation, and the closing one, is designed to take the threat out of the conversation. It helps the other person relax and view this as an issue the two of you are working to resolve as opposed to a battle one of you will win. It needs to be genuine. If you struggle to think of anything you can affirm, I often recommend affirming a possible positive future together, "I look forward to being able to enjoy working together."

    What can I affirm? How can I say it?

2. *Objective description of problem:* It is critical to stay objective and descriptive. When we drift into assumptions, judgments, or conclusions we drift into debatable territory. When we describe what happened to us and the impact, there is little room for argument.

This format is often helpful: When _____ happened, it had _____ impact. *"When you criticized me in front of the office I felt humiliated." "When the project was delayed it cost us an extra $100,000."*

Using the examples above, how can I describe this situation?

3. *Suggestion of solution:* This is a starting point. It might be accepted. It might not. If you relate to it as a starting point (as opposed to "take it or leave it") it can lead to a deeper exploration of options.

    Specifically describe what you are looking for. Example: *"I would like the office to hear an apology and for you to reiterate your confidence in my abilities." "I would like to be fully reimbursed for the additional costs."*

    What, specifically, do I want for a resolution? What are ideas about how that might be resolved?

4. *Exploration of options:* Be willing to explore different possibilities. I've been surprised at how often people walk away with better agreements than they were going to ask for—just because they used this process.

    The more time you spend understanding your own interests *and* the interests of the other person, the more likely you'll be able to find solutions that are mutually acceptable.

    What are your interests? What are theirs? What interests are shared? What solutions might meet those shared interests?

5. *Clarification of what you both agree the resolution looks like:* Absolutely critical. It is common that after a well-executed Step Two, the other party will reciprocate, and the sense of relief

will cause the parties to prematurely close the conversation. It's important to make sure you both understand what is agreed to. It is often wise to memorialize this in writing. This could range from an informal e-mail to a settlement agreement.

What format for clarification is the simplest and most appropriate for the context?

6. *A closing affirmation.* As discussed above. It helps remove threat from the conversation and solidifies the sense that you both are working together. This can be an affirmation about the current relationship, the potential relationship, or the possibility of a successful resolution. This should always be genuine: *"I like working here and I respect the passion that you have for our company." "This project is important to me as well and I'd like to see a successful conclusion for both of us."*

What can I honestly affirm? How can I say this?

Step Four: Clarify Where We Go from Here

In music there are two concepts that apply to conflict resolution. One is dissonance. The other is resolution.

Let's say I'm writing a song for guitar or piano and I want the song to create a sense of tension for an audience. I'll play what is called a dissonant chord. This is a variant of a chord that doesn't quite fit within the scale the entire song is set in. It contains notes that are a little off or jarring. Even though it is only a sound, just music, it generates an emotional response in the listener. Even if you aren't listening carefully, or don't understand music, a listener will often sense that something isn't right. The listener will naturally want and wait for resolution, this is created by something called a consonant chord, that creates a sense of conclusion or finality.

Usually, if a musician chooses to create a sense of dissonance they will later *resolve* this by playing the consonant chord, offering the listener an emotional conclusion. Sometimes, in songs that are edgy, trying to make a point, or trying to unsettle the listener, the musician will leave the chord *unresolved*. The music will stop playing, but the listener will have the experience of feeling like the song hasn't really ended. It wasn't complete, something hasn't been done.

The dissonance that is created in conflict can be so uncomfortable that people will often accept or pursue resolution too soon. Often, when people have confronted an issue, arrived at some level of acknowledgment or resolution, there is such a sense of relief that the conversation stops.

It's common for people to stop at Step Two—feeling like a cathartic release of frustrations and an apology resolved the problem. Others stop at Step Three—forgetting that trust needs to be rebuilt, that behaviors sometimes don't change immediately, that resentments sometimes reemerge.

We know this because, often, a short time after the conversation, one or both parties will discover that they are still carrying some unresolved emotion. They might not really feel trust toward the other person. Or they still don't feel respected or valued. Or they don't feel comfortable in the company of the other person. But now they don't know what to do. Because the issue was talked about. They thought it was resolved. But it's not.

If trust has been broken, it is rare that a single conversation will restore it. Often parties will need to time experiencing each other differently to rebuild trust. The same is true for respect.

It proves to be very helpful to go through the following questions to completely resolve the conversation.

Questions for Resolution

1. **Is there anything I need to put this issue behind me?** As a new mediator, I once worked with a lawsuit where one party, representing a business, tearfully apologized for what had happened to the litigant who had been a customer. I watched the anger wash from the

litigating party's face as she listened. She immediately said she was willing to drop her suit. There was a great sense of resolution on both sides as we drew up the settlement agreement that recorded this.

During a short break in the conversation, I was sitting alone with the former customer as the other party and their attorneys left the room to confer. I watched the anger begin to creep back into her tone and face. She began to talk about how she appreciated the acknowledgment but still wanted to take out full-page ads in the paper to warn the public and describe what had happened. As she talked, she grew angrier.

She followed through, in good faith, with the agreement she had made. But she didn't feel truly resolved.

She hadn't been clear to herself about what she needed to be able to leave the issue behind. By responding too quickly to the perception of resolution (the apology) she attempted to reciprocate with dropping her claim. All of which would be fine, but it didn't address an unmet need or desire that she still retained.

As a new mediator, I also was happy to have achieved a perception of resolution with a settlement agreement. Case closed. My work there was done.

I've learned, since then, to continue to probe when I notice that a party seems to not be able to completely set an issue aside. This contributes significantly to what I call a sustainable resolution.

Another way of looking at this: If a conflict is a wound in a relationship, just cleaning a lot of dirt out of the wound isn't sufficient to prevent reinfection. The whole thing needs to be cleaned out. Even when it is all cleaned out, there may still be a process of healing that is required.

A quick, "I'm sorry" may not be sufficient for rebuilding broken trust or restoring violated boundaries.

2. **Are there any changes to our relationship as a result of this situation? (If so, how can I respectfully and clearly communicate those?)**

It's best to detail any specific changes that may be needed. Let's say an employee has shown up late three times in a row for a client meeting. The account is lost. This creates a conflict. It also might mean that changes are required. What should those be?

As mentioned in Step Three, it helps to describe the path back to rebuilding trust. This allows the other party to gain a sense of how to change. This approach shouldn't be used for the purpose of manipulation or retribution. The changes in the relationship should be designed to create a path for repair. It's a service to yourself and the other person. If they know what to do, you've increased the likelihood that you'll achieve the result you hope for.

3. **What have I learned about myself and what I need to be able to relate well?**

We often miss important opportunities to grow because we fail to reflect. As a new mediator, I was working alone. My conversations were confidential. Because I was limited in the degree to which I could discuss my cases with anyone, I began a process. At the conclusion of each case, I conducted a sort of After Action Review. I would write out what I did, what approach seemed to work, what didn't seem to work, what I've learned, and what I wanted to try next time I faced a similar situation.

This process of self-reflection accelerated my learning. It helped me discover things, such as how my own desire to feel resolution can cause me to prematurely guide the parties to settlement.

In a conflict, it is easy to focus on what we've learned about the other parties. However, the emotional, even primal nature of conflict, often exposes our own emotional foundations. It is a rich opportunity to learn and grow.

4. **What have I learned about you and what you need to relate well?**
We learn about other people in conflict. If we work through these steps well, we often have the opportunity to learn about each other. We learn what the other person needs, wants, or prefers. We learn what our relationship needs. We might discover that boundaries are needed. We might learn about changes that are needed structurally in a workplace. Or culturally.

I recently met with a supervisor who was having problems with an employee. The employee originally was a great performer. However, the company quickly grew, and the needs changed. The expectations placed on her began to evolve. Over time, she was no longer performing to expectations. This lack of performance was blamed on her.

I encouraged the supervisor to first explore if perhaps the rules of the game had changed for the employee (Step Two). The employee still held the position that she had originally applied for and been hired into. For a number of years, her service had been exemplary. But recently, while her title stayed the same, the responsibilities and expectations had changed. This wasn't her doing.

Was there another role that she would be able to excel in? Without hesitation, her supervisor said, "Yes!" and identified a new position.

In another example, conflict has helped me learn about my wife. She benefits from time to process. Particularly, if there has been conflict between us. Early in our marriage, I interpreted the time she needed as avoiding the issue. My felt need to quickly get to closure or resolution seemed like pressure to her.

Over time, we've discovered that she often benefits (as it turns out, so do I) from getting time to think about things before responding. I benefit from knowing when we will revisit the issue. Reflecting on these questions has allowed us to learn these things about each other. This allows us to disagree (which will always be a part of our relationship) without the disagreement escalating into something unnecessary.

Setting the Stage for Success

Conflict is often a highly emotional experience (even if those emotions aren't immediately obvious). It may be tapping into other past emotions in our relationship or emotions from events altogether unrelated. As a result, it helps to prepare.

1. **Mental rehearsal shapes results.** Most people automatically rehearse a negative or combative conversation. It's no surprise that they often experience what they've imagined. Taking time to work through these steps on your own or with a coach can help. Take the time to imagine and work through a successful conversation. You can't control the other person. You can only control yourself.

2. **Follow through on Step Two.** This step is often the key to unlocking the dispute and turning it into a fruitful conversation.

3. **Don't delay.** It is important to find a good time to talk. However, when people are in conflict, there is a tendency to endlessly create reasons why no time is a good time. You probably will need to create a time to talk. You will also need sufficient time to talk deeply. Create this time.

4. **You've positively prepared, they probably haven't.** You've taken the time to read this, gain tools, shape your perspective positively. They are likely (not necessarily) still stuck in a place where they can only see this going poorly. If you are prepared to accept that they may not be as prepared as you emotionally or logically. Or that they may be well prepared to go to battle to win an argument—not to achieve resolution—you will be better able to relate to them more patiently and graciously.

5. **Allow the other person to respond and say what they need to say.** Listen, but don't react. Again, you've taken time to process a significant amount of what you feel. They likely haven't. There may be a lot of pressure that is coming out unfiltered. In many cases, the experience of being able to fully vent helps the other party move past some of the emotional blinders to a place of greater objectivity.

    Avoid reacting, agreeing, or disagreeing. This isn't always easy. But helps significantly. With an eye toward resolution, it is more effective to listen and then summarize what you've heard: "So, I hear that you feel (name the emotions they've communicated) because of (the situation they described.) Am I hearing you correctly?" or "I understand that you experienced (name the consequence they described) because of (name the situation or events they described)."

    This kind of reflective listening *does not* indicate that their interpretation of events is accurate, or fair or anything else. All you are doing is actively shifting the conversation to one where (A) They experience being fully heard by you and (B) You are gaining a better understanding of what is actually bothering them or what the issue is from their perspective.

6. **Consider time.** In most cases conflict, when unaddressed *does not* resolve. It festers and infects. However, sometimes it isn't possible or realistic to address or process everything all at once. If you are like me, you'd prefer to sit down and hash it all out at once. This can lead

to rash agreements that are more for the purpose of trying to relieve the tension than anything else. If you are like many other people, you may need more time to process and consider. While this can tend toward avoidance, it is often helpful to take a short, defined break. (Research has shown that a 20-minute break can dramatically impact the successful resolution of an argument between couples. This is attributed to the time it takes to process adrenaline and other stress hormones.) Either party may need more time, for various reasons. If trust has been violated or broken, time experiencing a different reality may be a necessary component of resolution. Allow the time. Just define when you will meet again.

7. **Stay safe.** These steps work well in most situations but if you feel threatened by the other person or unsafe, it may be wise to request that someone accompany you during the conversation, that a professional mediator help facilitate the conversation or, if need be, involve the appropriate authorities.

CHAPTER 6

Can't We All Get Along? Conflict in Relationships and Groups

Can't We All Get Along? Conflict in Relationships and Groups

If people spend enough time around each other, they should expect some disagreement, friction, or frustration to emerge. It is inevitable. However, when we maintain a perspective that Conflict is an Opportunity, we'll find that by exploring conflict can lead to improved communication, trust, ideas, and decisions.

How can a leader approach entering into conflict for the pursuit of resolution? Typically, leaders lean toward one of two options: wishing the issue away through denial or avoidance or trying to win through manipulation or coercion. Neither produces much value.

Denial

Denial often stems from black and white, all-or-nothing thinking. Conflict is believed to be bad. Because we aren't bad, we don't have conflict. That tense conversation? Not a conflict. That issue swept under the rug? No conflict here.

Early in my career, I was employed by an organization that had a strong culture of denial. They tended to believe that conflict = bad. If conflict was bad, only bad people (or people acting badly) experienced conflict.

In truth, a lot of quality and decent people worked here. But the belief that conflict was bad made it very difficult to express differing opinions. Meaningful debate or dialogue almost didn't exist. There wasn't trust that a needed confrontation could be accepted reasonably, so passive aggressive approaches were normalized.

I grew frustrated. The CEO, whom I had been close to, made a number of choices that felt unfair to me. Financial decisions that negatively impacted me, specifically, were never discussed. I allowed my attitude toward him to sour. I made comments that were inappropriate. I eventually resigned.

Sometime after leaving, I recognized my inappropriate attitude and the lack of resolution. I felt that I needed to address it. I felt he had been wrong, but I needed to just deal with my own contribution. I invited him to lunch. I wanted to discuss and apologize for the attitude I had and things I had said. Candidly, part of me also hoped he would acknowledge what he had done.

Instead he denied that I had ever copped an attitude. "You didn't do that," he said.

I was surprised. I tried again to engage the topic. Again, he said I didn't do anything. I began to realize that if he wouldn't allow me to own my own behavior, he wasn't in a place to recognize or own his own. I dropped the topic.

The consequence? Our relationship had a block in it. We can't be real. Our relationship has since atrophied to one of being amicable but distant acquaintances.

Avoidance

This approach to conflict is so common, and so recognizable, that many situational comedies will use the dynamic to drive their plot. Somebody makes a mistake, thinks they overheard something or is offended by someone. They spend the rest of the show avoiding addressing it head on. Or trying to fix something without anyone knowing. Or trying to figure out what someone is doing without just asking.

Avoidance usually comes from fear of *what if*? What if she gets angry? What if he quits? What if there is blowback? It is often the result of catastrophized thinking—naturally imagining and then preparing for worst case scenarios.

It can also come from not knowing how to manage personal emotions like anger or disappointment. I don't want to overreact, so I avoid a conversation. I don't want to appear vulnerable, so I don't mention an unfulfilled desire.

Manipulation

Avoidance can drift into manipulation. We manipulate when we attempt to influence or guide the choices of another. Manipulative behaviors are frequently excused or rationalized as being better than a feared, open disagreement. Enormously complex schemes can be created to try to change someone's behavior or choices because a direct conversation is viewed as too threatening.

An employee finds they aren't getting the hours they want. A vice-president discovers her budget has been cut. A policy is developed, impacting everyone, but targeting one or a few people. These are some forms of manipulation that result in moving the energy of the conflict. They don't resolve it.

Coercion

Coercion is forcing a choice. Or only offering one acceptable choice. A *because I told you so* approach to authority is often the most benign version of coercion. It can expand to various forms of belligerence, threats, or punishments if one's desires aren't understood and adhered to.

Don't misunderstand me. The words I used above can bring to mind a jowly, gruff CEO smoking a cigar deciding who he'll fire this week. However, they are just as often delivered with a smile, through an inspirational and popular leader. All of a sudden you realize that speaking up gets you kicked off this particular train.

As a leader, learning to address conflict as it emerges in groups is critical.

Ignoring It Doesn't Make It Go Away

Whatever our preferred forms for not dealing with conflict, or the relational dynamics of conflicts are, they all share something in common: Time and darkness don't make them go away.

People often argue this point almost compulsively. But what they nearly always are experiencing isn't resolution of the problem. It is just a diminishment of the sense of urgency or emotional intensity. This becomes obvious when a new offense occurs and triggers a reaction disproportionate to what just happened. Or a reaction that seems unfocused.

A laundry list of complaints that aren't necessarily related to each other, let alone whatever just happened.

In terms of a leadership role, it becomes important to be able and willing to address the animal in the room. Call it the elephant. Call it the 800-pound gorilla. Whatever.

Actively practicing working on your own approach to conflict will make it dramatically easier to help others as they relate to conflict—with yourself or with each other. However, the others may not be reading this book. So, what do you do when they are behaving poorly? Or, just don't know how to relate more effectively?

Sometimes They Just Need To Be Heard: Listening Well

When You Are Going in Circles

I was mediating a dispute some years ago. One of the parties was particularly agitated. Even though the other side's position was moving toward her in the negotiation, she kept bringing up the same topic. Just as we were about to come to agreement, we'd loop back to the beginning of the problem. We were going in circles.

I wondered if she didn't feel heard. Based on the conversation, it was clear to me that we were hearing and engaging with what she was saying. But the experience of going in circles is often due to someone not feeling validated on the point they are trying to communicate.

I stopped and said, "I'm hearing you say X." I paraphrased what I heard, using some of her own language. It was also the same information that we had been addressing in the negotiation.

She stopped and agreed. But I still didn't understand. I had no new information.

So, I asked her, "When you say X, does it also mean Y?"

"Yes!" She exclaimed. She elaborated a little more.

This was all new information. We were finally getting down to her underlying interests.

We had heard what she said. We had heard her positions. We hadn't heard the interests that made them important to her. What she really meant. Her suggested (really demanded) solution to the problem was one and the same with *why* it was important to her. But only she understood that.

Until I stopped to hear better.

What does it mean to be heard?

It is rarely enough for someone to know that you audibly heard them. They want a deeper sense that they are understood, valued, and respected. They want to know you understand their underlying interests. Interestingly enough, you'll often find that people have a higher level of tolerance for being disagreed with than they do for not being heard.

This need is often felt emotionally. Not logically. I don't *feel* heard. I may not understand why I'm so upset about an employee announcing (as opposed to asking) for a vacation on specific dates. I'll respond by talking about policies and so on. But underneath it, I *feel* disrespected. I *feel* like I or the team is devalued because someone didn't consider the impact of their decision on us.

So, I go on about policies. Or vacation days. Or deadlines. Or whatever. I often don't have the personal insight or courage to say, "When plans are made without considering their impact on others, it feels like you don't respect my authority. It also creates a lot of extra work for everyone else which makes me wonder if you value them."

The challenge is that many people don't have the patience to hear someone out. Or they feel a need to correct, defend, or otherwise challenge what is being said. Or they jump into their own story and start thinking about their own stuff. Or we listen to the surface without trying to understand what is underneath.

The Willingness to Hear

Our ability to hear begins with our attitude. I recently worked with a team and started to receive significant pushback to something I said. I had just gone over a bullet point summary of the decisions that they had made at a previous team meeting. It had been a tough meeting. But they made some breakthroughs. Developed some self-awareness. And came up with a list of priorities for change.

After presenting my summary, the group became resistant and defensive. Thinking I missed something, I backed up and tried again. I listed out the bullets of their conclusions on a white board. No change. They wouldn't accept what I was saying.

I stopped trying to explain my way through the defensiveness and decided to explore it instead. I didn't think it would be effective to say, "You guys seem pretty defensive." Instead, I made a small guess and shifted to the question of asking, "Did you feel that these bullet points (from the summary) were my personal analysis?"

They said, "Yes."

They felt heard. I now had better information. They had felt judged by me.

Their preexisting level of sensitivity and distrust was so high that any description of them, from an outside source, was open to being interpreted as an accusation. *Even if I was just repeating back their own words and decisions.*

Once they felt heard by me, I was then able to clarify that the points came directly from themselves. I reminded them of the conversation and the exercise that generated these points. They didn't reflect my own opinions.

When that was clarified, they noticeably relaxed. Even their physical posture changed. We then began productive problem-solving building on the previous work they had done.

We couldn't have gotten there if I hadn't stopped to hear what was behind the defensiveness.

How to Hear: Mirroring, Paraphrasing, Empathic Statements, Testing Meaning

Like everything else in this book, the process of hearing isn't linear. These tools aren't comprehensive. Trial and error should be expected. However, practicing will dramatically improve your conversations.

Mirroring

Using someone's own words can be very powerful. It almost seems too simple to be effective, but it is.

Imagine a scenario where you are working with a manager whom you supervise. He's very upset with his team's performance. Even to the point of planning to fire someone who was previously considered a star performer. Concerned, you've discussed the issue from a number of different angles. Solutions have been developed that seem acceptable and workable. But every time you move to close the conversation, he seems to get all worked up again.

Manager: "I can believe that his team isn't hitting their numbers. There is no excuse for this. When I was in his position, I would take my team and make them get there. I don't understand why he feels like he doesn't have to just do his job."

You (practicing mirroring): "Let me make sure I understand you: Their team isn't hitting their numbers and you don't feel this is excusable. When you had that role, you used to directly work with your team and make them get there. You don't understand why he isn't doing his job?"

Manager: "Exactly!"

Now, don't directly parrot back what was said, but you can use a lot of someone's own language. This is particularly helpful if you really don't understand why this is so important to them, or even what they mean.

Paraphrasing

Paraphrasing is the technique of repeating what you've heard in your own words. It can be very powerful in that it helps ensure that you understand what is being communicated. The risk is that you'll inject too much of your own interpretation into your word choices. If you have established trust, though, the other party will usually correct you. Your open response to that correction will usually contribute toward them feeling even more heard. Let's repeat the conversation above with paraphrasing.

Manager: "I can believe that his team isn't hitting their numbers. There is no excuse for this. When I was in his position, I would take my team and make them get there. I don't understand why he feels like he doesn't have to just do his job."

You (practicing paraphrasing): "Let me make sure I understand you— his team is underperforming and you don't understand why he's allowing it. Especially since when you were in his role you were able to achieve the performance you want now. Am I understanding you accurately?"

Paraphrasing is *very* helpful if someone has vented for a long time. Try to capture the primary, salient points and paraphrase them back. This can often be very helpful to someone who has a difficult time articulating. If you capture what they were trying to say, it isn't uncommon that they'll start using *your* language to communicate *their* thoughts.

I often blend the two. Paraphrasing for the benefit of brevity but mirroring specific language or phrases that seemed to carry specific meaning or weight. Even if I don't understand why.

I begin by introducing my intent: "Let me make sure that I understand you." "Or I want to make sure I'm hearing you correctly." The listener usually experiences this as, "I really want to hear you. I'm going to slow the conversation down just so that I've captured your words and thoughts accurately." It goes a long way toward people feeling well heard.

I will often follow up by saying some variant of, "Am I hearing you correctly?" or "Is there anything you would change or make sure is emphasized in what I said?"

Again, the person I'm speaking with experiences an often rare amount of attention on their thoughts. This goes a long way to helping them feel heard. If I've been mistaken, read into, or missed something it provides an opportunity that they'll often take to correct or expand my understanding. Additionally, it prevents them (particularly if they are very sensitive) from feeling judged. I've taken a stab at interpreting them. However, by asking for confirmation, I've left the final interpretation to them.

Empathic Statements

For our purposes, empathy is different than sympathy. Where sympathy might mean, "I feel your pain." Empathy might mean, "I can hear that this is very painful."

Sympathy is often dependent on our feelings. As a result, it is often mistaken (due to projection or transference.) Empathy is reflecting, nonjudgmentally, how they might be experiencing their situation.

I encourage that empathic statements be kept very short. *Do not start telling your own story about how you've been through something similar.* There are times when our story helps some people, usually if they feel very alone in their experience. Most of the time it feels like an intrusion on a conversation that is supposed to be about them.

In the scenario above, after I've mirrored or paraphrased, I might add: "That sounds like it must be very frustrating." Or "disappointing." Or "stressful." Or whatever seems to be the most appropriate.

Often, they'll respond with a "Yeah, it was really disappointing." But sometimes they'll say, "No, it wasn't really disappointing. I felt more betrayed after going out on a limb to get this person that position."

That's good. You've learned even more. You don't have to nail it with mind reading their emotions. You've indicated that you care, that it is having an emotional impact and you are still allowing them to own the story.

Testing Meaning

Testing meaning means I make an educated guess at what I think is bothering them and then ask for their confirmation or correction. This is what is demonstrated in both of my early examples. "I heard you say X (in this case mirroring) did you also mean Y (testing meaning)?" or "Did you feel that those bullet points were my analysis?"

In the case of the frustrated manager, I might ask something like, "Do you feel like their lack of performance reflects back on you?"

In both cases, I'm guessing at what might be underneath. But I'm asking about them and letting the person I'm speaking to own the final answer. Testing meaning can be a very effective tool for quickly getting beneath the surface to what is actually going on. However, it should be used carefully. If used poorly, people can feel judged, pigeonholed, or in other ways "not heard."

Be careful that you aren't layering in your own interpretation. Be careful that you aren't labeling or judging what is happening, instead this should be an exercise of open curiosity. Allow yourself to be very easily corrected.

Agreement Not Necessary

Hearing well doesn't mean that you agree. Because the experience of being heard is so validating, many people believe that allowing someone to express their views is tacit agreement or validation. That isn't our objective. We listen well to validate the person and to better understand where they are coming from.

Once you've let go of the need to agree with everything around you, the easier it will be to hear others. Ironically, the less you need agreement, the easier it will often be to find agreement.

Sometimes They Really Don't Know Anything Different: Structured Coaching

I recently had a meeting with a supervisor in the construction industry. He's dealing with issues on his team. "I've spent my whole career avoiding issues like this. I just ran the equipment and did the work. I didn't care what others did."

He liked his job. But I had to remind him, his job was people now. Instead of building or maintaining physical things, his job included building people and maintaining relationships.

Those weren't part of his job description. It wasn't part of what he was hired to do. But you cannot take on a leadership role without discovering that you work through people. They need to operate well. To do that they need to relate well. They often don't know how.

So, we coach. We help them grow. Here are three concepts that will support effective coaching.

Listening and Issue Identification

One of the most effective set of tools in conflict coaching is the ability to:

- Listen well.
- Help others identify individual issues and relevant parties.

In conflict, most people don't feel well listened to. Usually for good reason. Simply taking the time to allow someone to "get their air out" can be powerfully helpful. Often more helpful than giving advice.

A significant percentage of the population tends to think better out loud. Talking helps them process their thoughts. So, it's important to help them get all (or many) of their thoughts out. It is also important to not waste time analyzing or correcting their thoughts. At least not at this point. They just need to dump them out to see what they are.

While you are listening, pay attention to *emotions* that seem to be expressed. Look for associated issues that seem particularly important or relevant to those emotions. By using the listening tools discussed earlier, you can help them discover what they are really feeling and what makes this important to them.

It helps to separate out different issues and parties. Conflicts tend to get balled together and named as a single issue. *The problem I have with the wholesale department.* That is a nonspecific description that doesn't allow anyone to know what is going on. *Who,* specifically, is the problem with? *What,* specifically, is the problem? Is there actually more than one problem? Is each problem connected to the same people? If not, which problems are connected to which people?

This information is enormously helpful. It helps to shape a strategy for approaching a resolution process. It, also, often deescalates someone.

It isn't uncommon for someone to say, "Wholesale act like ignorant jerks. They can't seem to get an order right. But every time I call them they act condescending toward me."

Most frequently, the problem is narrowed down to one or a few people filling orders. Not the *whole* wholesale department. As the individual you are talking to begins to recognize this, they sometimes begin to see things more proportionately. They may also begin to start to see solutions.

Using the Four Steps

Use the four steps to resolution to coach:

> *Step One: Clarify What They Really Want:* Through listening as described above, help the person you are talking to define what they really want. I often ask the question, "What does fixing this look like to you?" or "What would a good solution look like to you?"
>
> They most often aren't sure, so we take some time to explore this.
>
> Helping them get clear on what they want and why that is important to them helps you gain perspective on where you need to focus to achieve resolution.
>
> *Step Two: Encourage Them to Own Their Part (if any):* In nearly all disputes there is a tendency to deny, minimize, or justify our own

poor behavior. If someone has acted in a way that contributes to the problem, it helps to identify this and work with them to identify an appropriate approach.

As stated before, there is nearly always resistance at this point. People often don't want to accept that they had a part to play. Depending on the openness of the person I'm talking to, sometimes it makes more sense to temporarily set aside Step Two, look at Step Three, and then come back to Step Two.

I don't force the issue. But I do encourage that it be explored. Again, I do this because it is nearly always that case that both sides have contributed to the creation, maintenance, or expansion of the conflict *and* because when either of the two sides is willing to acknowledge their part, the other side will often reciprocate and resolution is nigh.

Don't force this point but put it out there. The person(s) on the other side of the conflict is often more than willing to shed light on how they felt judged, missed, or in some other way wronged by the person you are coaching. You'll often have the opportunity to go back and explore the Step Two.

Step Three: Help Them Ask for What They Want

Most people struggle to define or articulate what they want. As a result, they spin their wheels in the attempt to find some kind of satisfaction or resolution. One of the great services you can provide is to help them articulate what they want. I often ask, "What does fixing this look like to you?" or "How would you know that this issue has been resolved?"

In most cases, it takes people some time to formulate their answer. And that is exactly where you want them to be. In the place of getting clear about their actual desires.

When people respond, they will nearly always respond positionally. "I would like to be repaid what I'm owed." Or "I want him to be fired." Or "I think they should change their policy."

Often, the positions offered aren't very specific or realistic: Once I was told, "I want him to be very happy, very far away from here."

Resolution is rarely found by engaging the position. What I often do is keep digging for the underlying *interests*. The following questions can help with this:

"What does that solution mean to you?"

"What makes that important/valuable to you?"

"What if that doesn't happen? What are you concerned might happen?"

Following this, help them think through multiple solutions or options that might be acceptable to them. This is always an interesting process because, in conflict, most people become very black and white in their thinking. They have one solution that they want and anything else is perceived to be a compromise.

However, I have often found that by trying to expand the list of possible options it is *frequently* possible to discover solutions that are even more attractive to both parties. If nothing else, you are positioning them to more effectively negotiate for what they want.

Once they've clarified what they want and why it is important to them—as well as some of the options they may be open to—I will often help them practice having this conversation. I use the Step Three template described previously.

I usually ask them to either write it out or discuss it with me. Then it is often very helpful to work through it as a role play. The role play is easy because the characters are known and they now have a script.

If we leave most people to just wing it, they will nearly always slip back into their initial emotional state and positions. By so doing, they often sabotage their own efforts toward resolution. By practicing this in a role play, you have an opportunity to work with them regarding words or tone that may trigger or escalate additional conflict. You can help them become more comfortable with the idea of and pathway to actual resolution.

Believing it is possible is an important part of making it possible.

Step Four: Help Them Clarify Where They Go From Here

This may or may not take place all in one conversation. Because of the emotion that may be involved in the dispute there is often a corresponding sense of relief when it appears that resolution has happened. As discussed earlier, this sense of relief is not an indicator that true, sustainable resolution has been arrived at. The goals of coaching Step Four include:

- Preventing someone from accepting a false resolution that won't be sustainable
- Helping someone get clear and honest about they need to move ahead
- Clarifying what is needed for trust to be rebuilt
- Establishing or reinforcing healthy boundaries

Sometimes They Aren't in Control of Themselves: Changing the Environment

When I first began working in Kosovo, first responsibility, before I started working with housing reconstruction, was to start a couple of therapeutic preschools. We were targeting young children who had lived during the war and likely experienced war trauma, as we called it then.[1]

One of the schools I founded was in a community comprised of the Roma and Egyptian minorities.[2] In this community we began with two different classes of preschool students. One was the Green class and the other was the Pink class. Students had been randomly assigned to their classes, so there was no obvious difference between the two. They met at separate times but shared the same teacher, Ibrahim.

One of the classes began to regularly experience disruptive behaviors with the children. Ibrahim was at a loss for how to control the behavior. He asked that I help.

Through working with Ibrahim and observing the classes, we discovered that the behaviors started up after a particular play time each day. During this play time, toys were brought out. One boy seemed to find the toys overstimulating and would begin to act inappropriately. Not knowing how to share, he would get excited and start fights. This would trigger negative responses in the other children. The rest of the day was, routinely, a struggle.

---

[1] 9/11 happened toward the end of my year in Kosovo. It was 9/11 that brought a stronger awareness of post-traumatic stress and the term PTSD to the common vernacular.

[2] The Egyptian community had no relationship with modern day Egypt. However, oral history referenced their origin as being from Egypt.

We discussed intervention options with the one child. We considered appropriate forms of redirection or discipline. We discovered, upon reflection, that this community was so poor that almost no children owned their own toys. So, by introducing toys, we had introduced objects of desire and levels of stimulus that we hadn't intended. We basically weren't sure what to do.

Eventually, we realized that of all the things we were there to do, teaching the children to share wasn't an urgent priority. Important, but not at the expense of other objectives. Instead of developing a disciplinary strategy we decided to experiment with something else.

We decided to just change the environment.

We never mentioned the toys. Never addressed the behaviors. But before the next class, we removed the toys. We replaced them with fun, physically active games. The children never seemed to notice that their toys were gone.

The behavior of the entire classroom changed. The one child didn't act out anymore. He didn't trigger the other children. We no longer needed to deal with disruption. The children could focus.

For the well-behaved class, we made no changes at all. They were never needed.

The lesson stuck with me. Sometimes our environments create friction. Sometimes our systems and policies create tension. Sometimes the physical space, or elements therein, provokes conflict.

Yes, it would be great if in the normal workplace, everyone we worked with was consistently well-rested, emotionally intelligent, patient, kind, and considerate. But not only is everyone else not that way, we're not either.

Now, when I do my consultations with clients, I look at environmental factors along with everything else. In fact, the environmental changes are often the easiest wins for a leader: The low-hanging fruit; simple things like putting up white boards that list individual priorities; changes to shift schedules; increasing the amount of face-to-face meetings; and putting policy documents online.

Sometimes, the best leadership is less like hockey and more like curling. Less slapping of the puck into the goal, and more sweeping the ice to encourage the motion of the stone.

Sure, hockey players attract more attention. But curlers can still be Olympians. And they keep all their teeth.

Sometimes They are Toxic: When and How Removal Can Be an Act of Service

I lean toward helping people retain their jobs. It's a big deal to discuss a termination. But sometimes it is needed. Despite media portrayals of callous employers, I find that most leaders are more likely to avoid letting people go for too long. This is very often the case in terms of dealing with toxic people.

It may not seem this way at first, but timely termination can be an act of service.

For our purposes, I define a toxic person as someone who behaves in a way that works against the best interests of other and the success and harmony of the team.

A toxic person is not likely to be intentionally toxic. They don't wake up thinking, "How can I undermine progress and make life unbearable for others today?"

Instead, this person has a way of relating that seems to erode the health of the whole. Their influence is often subtle. Their impact may take place over time. Their poison is often bundled within very desirable skills, strengths, or qualities.

A toxic person is rarely overt in how they damage the workplace. They are usually subtle. Nuanced.

Typically, they are just people who don't know how to relate to other people and circumstances well. They often find ways to frame themselves (with varying levels of persuasiveness) as victims. However, often, they also have the ability to be overbearing, controlling, and demanding. In fact, they can be outright abusive.

There is a myriad of ways that someone can be toxic. However, they all share two key differentiating factors:

They are unwilling or unable to see their behaviors and attitudes as damaging.

They are unwilling or unable to change.

This doesn't mean that if they are confronted they won't recognize they are in trouble. But they are far more likely to interpret whatever happens as, ultimately, someone else's fault. In rare cases where they appear to see that they are having a damaging impact, they might gush with contrition, apologies, and promises. You might even see short-term adjustments in behavior.

But this is about getting you off their back. Not about starting a personal journey of self-awareness, change, and growth. It won't be long before their toxicity is felt somewhere else.

Get rid of these people.

I've found that workplaces will tend to hold on to toxic people, sometimes for years. They will hold on to these people even when they directly contribute to the turnover of other, great employees. They will hold on to them even when they depress the effectiveness and undermine the moral of those who remain.

Toxic people have the ability to cause leaders to reframe the situation away from "How is this one person undermining the happiness, health, and effectiveness of our whole team?" to "I'd hate to let this person go, they are going through such a hard time at home right now." Or "But in this certain area they are high performers." Or "But they have been so loyal and we've worked together for so long."

Of course, they are having a hard time at home. They are toxic there as well.

The value of their individual performance is neutralized if they are dragging down the performance of others.

They are *not* loyal if they are focused on themselves and unable or unwilling to change destructive behaviors.

Over the last couple of years, a significant number of my clients finally faced and let go of toxic people in their environment. To a person, these toxic employees were: in leadership positions, had been around a long time, were very intelligent, and competent.

They looked great on paper.

In *every case* when these people were let go, the organizations experienced a lift. A lift in morale, a return of employees that had left and an increase in profits. It was amazing to see how single individuals were able to hold entire organizations back.

Not only this, but in half of these situations, it was discovered (after the fact) that these, "very committed, very loyal" people were engaged in unethical and illegal behavior including active deceit, withholding or stealing bonuses or awards from subordinates, falsifying records, and embezzlement.

It is an act of service to your team, to everyone else, to protect them from toxic people. It is an act of service to ensure that people who are unwilling or unable to change are not allowed to continue to prey on others.

It is also an act of service to the toxic person. While it will be rare, there are occasions where their removal will be the sufficiently cold bucket of water that will spark long overdue self-reflection and change. It can be the thing to finally help them move to a path that will eventually allow their success.

But in the meantime, don't tolerate toxicity. When you begin to see signs of it, address it quickly. Confront the behaviors. Describe the impact.

If they are unable or unwilling to see what you've described, watch closely. If you see a pattern, let them go.

If they *do* see what you've described but are unwilling or unable to change (even with support like coaching or mentoring or training) let them go.

As stated elsewhere in this book, I recommend a stepped approach.

First go and talk to them, objectively address the behavior and the consequences.

Be very clear what *fixing it* looks like. Toxic people can be exceptional at riding the line and pushing boundaries. Describe the precise positive behaviors you are hoping to see. You may discuss but shouldn't have to explain all the negative behaviors you don't want to see. It's not your job to re-parent them.

Second, if they don't respond or acknowledge what you are saying, bring in a witness to the behavior. See if they will respond to more than one person saying, "When you do X, Y happens. And that hurts people, impacts team performance, and needs to change."

If they still don't respond, let them go. Don't prolong these processes. In most cases it should take no more than 30 to 90 days for people to demonstrate sufficient change in behavior for you to know they are genuinely trying.

Trust, usually, take longer to regain. But you should be able to tell, quickly, if they are making an effort to rebuild trust.

If you are in a position where you have the authority to discipline or terminate, and you are wrestling with the same person for longer than three to six months, you now share responsibility for the problem.

In the instances where there may be a more complex or involved termination process, there may be a slightly longer time frame. But you get my point. If a toxic person is tolerated or endured by leadership, leadership is choosing to allow toxicity in the workplace. Leadership now shares culpability.

CHAPTER 7

Driving on the Wrong Side of the Road: Using Structures and Systems to Build Good Conflict

I love driving in foreign countries. It's an immediate way to gain insight into another culture. It opens the doors to experiences otherwise unavailable.

It's also little like being in a video game. (Don't tell the other drivers I feel that way!)

I remember first driving in Nairobi, Kenya. They follow the British system and drive on the left side of the road. It's a small difference. But it influences nearly every action from there on. All the automatic habits that I've built up over the years will now only cause problems. Everything from how the vehicle is set up, to where to look for signs, to how to signal turns.

In Nairobi, they have a fantastically large roundabout. I love it. I think it is six lanes wide. Since we have nothing like this in my city, there was a small sense of "uh oh" as I approached it the first time.

It looked intimidating. But it really wasn't that big of a deal. I just learned the system. And it works.

Here's the deal. I've driven in lots of countries. Some countries drive on the left. Others drive on the right. Some rely heavily on traffic signs and lights. Some rely heavily on hand gestures, and honking, and shouting.

When I first started working in Kosovo, the society was in a state of near anarchy. People drove wherever they wanted. This was in part because the roads were so bad. It was also, in part, because they could. I remember, one day, watching a police car drive backward through traffic. It wasn't necessary. But he could do it. So, he did.

However, even in Kosovo, there was a system. A way that traffic worked. It was very informal. And the rules kept changing. But it was easier to drive when I learned it.

As a driver, I have found that learning the local system (as opposed to insisting on my own system) was the fastest way to become both confident and safe on the roads. I noticed that people who never wanted to learn a local system also rarely ever drove. Their experience in the country was severely limited as a result.

What Are Structures and Systems?

Experts split hairs on the definition of organizational structures and systems. Here's what I mean: Structures and systems are the parts of town, roads, bridges, highways, bike trails, signs, lights, laws, and law enforcement that make up your transportation system.

Structures are the major components of your organization perhaps defined as production, wholesale, retail, administration, sales and service. The specifics might be different for your organization. Systems are how all of those things connect to and work with each other. Both internally and externally. For the purposes of this topic, I'm also included things like processes, procedures, and policies in the words structures or systems.

Roads are systems. A road network connects parts of a community with each other. It connects one community to another. Well-designed road systems improve traffic efficiency and reduce accidents.

My office overlooks a frontage road, which runs alongside a highway. The frontage road is one-way. Nearly all the local roads that feed into the frontage road do so with a T intersection. T intersections, on one-way roads, are usually very easy to navigate. There are very few options.

However, there was one T intersection just south of my office that used to account for a high amount of traffic accidents.

My guess is that when it was originally designed, it worked fine. But as the city grew, more traffic started to move through the system.

There was also a tempting on-ramp to the highway that ran right in front of the intersection. Technically, you couldn't access it from the T intersection. But if you were motivated enough, you could surely try.

Kind of like the old video game of *Frogger*. Not everyone made it across the road.

So, the municipality had some choices:

- They could ignore it. After all, it isn't their problem if people want to run into each other.
- They could pay for constant police presence, to ensure caution, and enforce good driving behavior.
- They could tighten up standards for driving licenses and force drivers using that road to go through Driver's Ed and retest for their license.
- They could change the system.

They chose to change the system. After a few months of construction, we had a brand new…T intersection. But they made a few important changes. The angles of the T were slightly different. The on-ramp to the highway had been moved to a less tempting location. Visibility for oncoming traffic was improved.

The accidents disappeared. Gone.

Do you see the workplace correlation?

Sometimes, when a workplace is struggling with conflicts, it's worth looking for patterns. Most workplace conflicts are blamed on personalities. However, very often it is an individual personality responding poorly to an issue in the system. This issue will create patterns of problems. If you see a pattern of conflict, run a check on processes or systems that may influence that pattern.

A one-time fix of the system is worth far more than a hundred employee counseling sessions.

Structures and Systems Are Important

Structures and systems are important. Once an organization has moved through an entrepreneurial phase, the primary approach for maximizing its profits or accomplishments is through either efficiencies or scaling existing efforts. Efficiency is largely obtained by taking anything that is done regularly and making it as simple and predictable and as easy to access as possible. Then regular users don't have to use extra resources, brainpower, or energy to navigate it. New users have a simpler learning curve.

When something breaks in the system, because there is consistency, it becomes easier to diagnose and either repair or improve on.

The Human Nature of Structures and Systems

Because of the natural human tendency to get lazy, we all tend to build habits. In organizations, these habits often become systems. "The way we do things." As a result, we often do things the way we do due to institutionalized accident. Not design.

I don't have the ability to design to road systems in Nairobi (or anywhere else, for that matter). In those contexts, I just have to learn and accept the system that is.

However, as a leader, I am an architect of structure and systems. I need to own my role in it. As I do, I am empowered to reduce unhealthy conflict.

Key Systems in Most Organizations

Just like the human body, an organization is comprised of numerous systems.

However, it is unlike a healthy human body, which is conceived with a genetic blueprint of these systems and predictably develops the same systems, from one human to another. In the human body, systemic or structural variance is rare and usually deadly.

Instead, most organizations develop in a truly organic way, often with unpredictable results.

When organizations are small or are in a heavy startup phase, *heavy* systemization is counterproductive and onerous. However, *appropriate* systems and structures are still necessary for growth. As a rule, any system that is adopted should result in overall lift in an organization. It should result in increased effectiveness, efficiency, and reduced conflict.

Very small businesses, start-ups, or very fast growth organizations often don't have well developed systems. They are often not needed, no one feels they have time to build them or by they time they are developed they are no longer relevant. However, when these organizations struggle, it is often an indication of a structural failure—either the lack of structure, one that was cut and pasted from another organization, one that hasn't grown with the organization, one that isn't maintained or reinforced or something else.

Typical Organizational Structures & Systems

Here are examples of structures and systems that most organizations (even small ones) should have in place.

Leadership and Management Systems

Planning, decision making/reporting, training, leadership development, and performance management.

Operational Systems

Financial management, production, administration, technology, and health and safety.

Distribution and Customer Service Systems

Marketing, sales, product/service delivery, payment, customer service, account management.

Operationally, my consulting business is small. It's considered a "micro-business." However, small doesn't not mean without complexity.

I employ myself and contract an assistant, a bookkeeper, an accountant, a web master, and designers. Additionally, I usually have a business coach. I have to manage all of them. Some of them come with their own systems or processes which makes the relationship easier. For others, they need to be developed.

Additionally, I typically carry six to twelve consulting and coaching clients at any given time. With some clients, I only interact with one person. With others, I interact regularly, with dozens of people. Just to engage with my clients includes the structures of our engagement, the processes I use there as well as managing all my technology (phone, internet, scheduling software, etc.)

Along with serving my current clients, I need to keep an eye on my pipeline. So, I have processes for marketing, prospecting, sales conversations, and contracting.

And the lists can go on. As I write them out, it seems like a lot. But in reality, most of them hum along in the background with little to no effort at all. The ones that take effort, I've often delegated out to others.

I utilize or interact with many of the aforesaid systems, because it makes me more effective, by allowing me and others to work more efficiently and it reduces potential conflict between the players.

In fact, one of the differences between solo-consultants who achieve a significant level of success and those who are struggling is the ability to develop systems. It frees me up to do what only I can do. I can hire others do the rest.

It frees me up to build a business that doesn't require that I constantly have to exchange time for money. It prevents conflict because it improves communication. When conflict occurs, it is often possible to quickly resolve it by examining where a breakdown happened within the system. This avoids inaccurate and unnecessary personal judgments.

Growth, for most organizations, is only possible or sustainable with development of systems. Large organizations that work in multiple locations are only able to consistently replicate results and customer experiences by designing structures and systems.

As a consultant, I've found that a very high percentage of workplace conflict can be explained and resolved by addressing organizational systems.

Formal and Informal Systems

One of the key and most critical lenses that you can use is the ability to recognize the difference between *formal* and *informal* systems.

You've most likely had the experience of being hired into a position, going through an orientation on the company, your job, expectations, policies, procedures, and so on. Then, after you started at work, you start to learn, "What you need to do to really get things done around here." This is when you discover how things really work. The people you really should talk to if you need a decision, or want a change or require support.

Typically, the higher up you move within an organization, the more important it is to know how things really work.

What is being described here is the difference between *formal* and *informal* systems. The formal being the official policies, procedures, and lines of authority. The informal being the invisible ones that decisions and power and influence tend to flow through.

This is easy to see. Imagine getting together with three other friends for game night. Let's say the four of you choose to play Monopoly. Two of the friends, including the host, play Monopoly together all the time. You are also experienced with the game but have never played with this group. The fourth friend has never played at all and needs to be introduced.

Because rules are boring, everyone else orients the fourth friend with a basic overview that goes like, "Let's just jump in. You'll figure it out as we go."

As you play, you start to discover that there are house rules that the host and his friend know and insist on. These are exceptions to the normal rules or they fill in blanks in areas that the normal rules don't cover. It starts to appear that the house rules are typically only remembered and introduced at moments when the host or his friend seems to benefit in some way.

In real-life scenarios (and in most Monopoly games that I've played), this is what starts to destroy the game and the evening. Based on how hard it is to get people to play Monopoly, it's my guess that many other people have experienced this as well. The game of Monopoly doesn't inherently create conflict. But conflict is often created because of a lack of agreement, or equal access to and familiarity with the rules.

There are many theories as to why two systems, formal and informal, emerge or are reinforced. The following is a list of frequent causes:

- An entrepreneurial, innovative, fast change culture often doesn't lend itself to formalization
- A maturing company prefers the freedom of the entrepreneurial experience and views formal structure as unnecessary weight or bureaucracy
- Poorly designed or reactive policies or procedures that allowed to remain due to organizational inertia

- Leadership who don't exercise the discipline to follow their own rules
- Leadership who realize that if the rules to internal success are mysterious and closely held, they retain more power
- Leadership who are uncomfortable with setting and maintaining boundaries

As a general rule, the closer the alignment between the *formal* and *informal* the healthier and more effective an organization will be. The more divergence exists between the two, the unhealthier the organization will be.

In most cases, the reasons for why divergence exists are less important than the answer to the question, "Why is it allowed to remain now?" Whatever the initial cause, the two systems are usually allowed to remain because it empowers, "those who know how the game is really played." It is a way of consolidating control.

In many cases, this enforcement of the informal system won't necessarily be intentional. It's mostly people just doing what seems easiest. But this doesn't prevent it from being damaging.

This isn't to say that you won't find very large, robust, long-lasting organizations with highly divergent cultures. You will. In fact, it is probably more common to have divergence. However, the more divergence you have, the more energy and efforts are diverted from productive work and results.

If you run your workplace the way many people play Monopoly, you can expect people with options to not want to play with you.

Troubleshooting

When asked to address an organizational conflict, I will often begin with an assessment of an organization's systems. This assessment might be very informal, just asking questions and observing. Or it might be a more formal process. Either way, I'm looking for patterns. Patterns are the lights on the dashboard.

A Pattern of Symptoms

Systems develop when some kind of activity or decision needs to be done on a regular basis. When they work well, they produce consistently desirable results.

When they work poorly you often see strain in one or more of the following areas: efficiency, effectiveness, or relationships.

When beginning an engagement with an organization, I stay alert for patterns in these areas. If there is conflict in a workplace, I specifically look for answers to this question, "Is this conflict genuinely unique and abnormal in this organization?" If it is, then it may not be systemic. It may be tied more directly to the individuals involved. However, if the conflict we're addressing is one that occurs regularly, when it is reasonable to begin exploring if there is something systemic that is either (a) generating, (b) magnifying, or (c) allowing the problem to exist.

Triggers

Once I discover a pattern, I will often look for what seems to trigger it or set it off. Does this issue happen each time there is a promotion in this department? Does this issue happen at the beginning of a particular season? Then I dig deeper.

If a promotion seems to trigger the problem, are there underlying triggers, such as how someone is promoted? Or how this decision is communicated? Are there always the same person/people involved?

If problems always emerge in the middle of a busy summer construction season, is this when they actually were started? Are they actually triggered by hasty hiring or orientation decisions when bringing in summer crews? Possibly the problems started when projects grew beyond a certain size and had less direct oversight? The consequences of problems may emerge quite some time after the initial triggers of the problem.

The Highest Level of Direct Leadership

I look for the highest level of leadership that has direct impact on the situation. This doesn't necessarily mean the highest level of leadership within the organization. But I want to work with the all the decision makers who most directly shape the conditions that we are trying to change. There are a couple of reasons for this. The first is that most change is easier if you have leadership involved in the change process.

The second is that if this situation has continued for some length of time, it is part of the environment that the leader has either created, actively maintained, or passively allowed.

For example, I once worked with a manager who oversaw several supervisors and work teams. The problems I was asked to intervene with were occurring at the work team and supervisory level. As we explored the issues, I began to notice that a number of the practices and decisions that were irritating the situation were coming from senior leadership. It wasn't that they were directly causing problems, but they weren't paying attention to the downstream impacts of their leadership. In this particular organization, among other things, I discovered a very low willingness to confront problems and a correlating lack of accountability for workplace behavior and performance.

At the most senior level, it was interpreted as "We don't micromanage" or "We really try to trust people here." The truth is, senior leadership tended to avoid conflict and wouldn't provide accountability. Additionally, they had allowed an informal structure to develop. It wasn't as if they were acting unethically or breaking the law. But a tone was set that, "If you want to, you can get away with poor performance here." This manifested in insubordinate behavior, low productivity, turf politics, and so on.

For me to only intervene directly with the teams would achieve very little. My intervention needed to focus on senior leadership.

There Are No Monsters Under Your Bed

When I was young, I somehow discovered that monsters lived under my bed. I don't know how this seems to be such a universal experience. It sure was mine. I did figure out that if I pulled the blanket completely over me I'd be safe. Unfortunately, the air under the blanket would get stale very quickly. I didn't have a monster snorkel, so I'd have to risk creating a small opening to breathe through. Risky business.

In organizations the words *systems* or *change* spark similar responses from leadership. Immediately, the "what ifs?" begin their attack. What if people don't accept this? What if it creates conflict? What if it derails us? What if we're exposed to risk? What if it changes our culture? What if we lose what we've invested so much to build? What if?

We pull the blanket over our collective leadership heads. We deny that we're doing this by pointing to the tiny openings we've created to breathe through.

As a child, I could spend hours locked in this invisible battle with the monsters under my bed. As an adult, with small children, I can spend hours trying to persuade my children that the monsters don't exist, that there are no monsters in the room or I'd never let a monster get them.

Or, I can just turn on the lights.

Well...sometimes there actually is something under your bed.

And, in truth, sometimes there actually is something there. But you should still turn on the lights and look. It won't be a monster.

In most cases, it'll be something as terrifying as a dust bunny. So, a real thing you don't want there or want to deal with. But usually not truly threatening or catastrophic.

And...turning on the lights doesn't create the monster or the dust bunny. It just lets you see what is actually there, so you can deal with it.

How to Face the Monsters Under Your Bed (Or Just Change The Systems)

Use as Much Light as Possible

Life isn't always easy. Problems, setbacks, conflict, and even catastrophes happen. However, the *biggest* problems most people face are the ones we imagine. We tend to exaggerate and catastrophize more due to *what might be* as opposed to *what is*. Because we are talking about systems, what we find is usually not that scary.

Get Help

It is much easier to face a challenge, when you have someone with you. There are two kinds of helpers you should look for. The first is just someone who cares about you and believes in what you are trying to do. Whether a business partner, a team member, a loyal employee, a spouse... whomever. The second is someone who is good at dealing with whatever might be there. This should *always* be someone who has successfully dealt with similar issues before. This might be an experienced friend or mentor. It might be a paid coach or consultant. Having either or both will make a real difference.

Commit to Dealing with Whatever You Find

The best way to deal with issues is to fully commit. This prevents small problems from growing. It usually reduces overall cost. It usually makes it a lot easier. Difficult, undesirable, unwanted work is just that. It all gets easier when we just commit to completing it well.

CHAPTER 8

I Can't See What You Are Saying: Why Culture Is So Powerful and How to Shape It

Culture is to people what water is to fish. It is everywhere, it is necessary, we use it to propel ourselves forward and navigate. We can't move or function without it...but we don't notice it. In fact, we won't notice it at all until there is change.

Everyone experiences culture, but most have a difficult time recognizing it or describing it. I was working with a group of Alaska Native leaders as they were trying to define and identify culture as one of their core values. One of the leaders stood up and said, "This is just what we do. It isn't something we can define."

Directly after high school I moved to Mexico for a while. When I returned, my first job was as a delivery driver for an auto body supply store. In a conversation with the owner about the differences between cultures, he made one of those I-know-what-I'm-talking-about-because-I'm-the-owner statements, "America has no culture." End of that conversation.

Despite what he said, as leaders, it is important that we are able to see' our own cultures and learn to intentionally build and maintain ones that best serve our organizations. The better you can recognize your culture, the better you can intentionally shape it. The more effectively you can lead within it.

What Culture Is and Why You Don't Get It

Geert Hofstede, a notable scholar in the fields of cultural and organizational dynamics, has conducted one of the most comprehensive studies

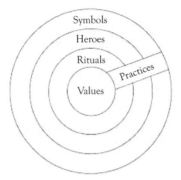

Figure 8.1 The "onion" metaphor of culture

relating to culture and its impact on organizations. He uses the picture of an onion to help people think of culture (Fang 2010). (See Figure 8.1.)

The Outer Layer (Symbols)

On the outside of the onion there is what most people describe as culture: The way people dress, the language they use, the music they listen to, the food they eat. This is what you first notice (consciously or subconsciously) when you walk into a workplace or job site. Are people wearing suits? Are they in jeans? Are they in uniforms? Are they moving fast? Or do they seem to move slowly? Do they seem serious or are they joking? Are they formal in their language or casual? Do they show obvious deference to rank or is it more difficult to know who the leader is? This is the surface of culture.

The Middle Layers (Heroes and Rituals)

Organizations will have developed their *Heroes*. How Heroes are defined can tell you a lot about their culture. Some organizations are heavily focused on specific founders or strong leaders. In others, these leaders are less obvious, and they might look to identify heroes among employees. Some look to history. Others prefer contemporary heroes.

In any of these cases, a hero will tend to embody a sense of the ideal for that culture.

Rituals have to do with common experiences that everyone will have. Rituals are expected patterns of behavior or ways of relating, usually tied to an event. The common onboarding experiences. How rewards or acknowledgments are conferred. Events that bond the team or organization. Even how difficulties are dealt with can be ritualized.

Organizational rituals can tell you about the values of an organization. To make up an extreme example: Organization A only pays for company celebrations when a new contract is secured. Organization B only pays for company celebrations on birthdays and common holidays. Both reflect different values.

Organization A may seem like it accomplishes more because of its emphasis on performance. However, it may not be sufficiently building the relational strength and social capital that buoy performers through challenging times. It may leave people in isolation or fostering unhealthy competition between supposed team members.

Organization B might seem like the more caring place to work. That is, unless you need to accomplish something or rely on the high performance of others. Then you start to experience conflict and friction because the culture is not performance oriented.

The Core Layer

The core is where Key Beliefs or the shared world view reside. I once heard this described as a Truth Box. It's a place where we *just know* that certain things are true about life, reality, what's truly important, and how things really work. We place them in our Truth Box and never reconsider or examine them.

It's this core that informs a culture if conflict is innately dangerous, sinful, or wrong—or an opportunity for growth and better understanding. It's this place where we believe people can be trusted or we need to protect ourselves. It's here where we hold the code to how we define success or accomplishment. The core layer is, most often, unexplored.

Many organizations will poke around at it, a little, when they establish organizational values and so on. However, they often don't explore or challenge value dissonances. Let's say excellence is identified as a value. We discover how true or core that is when it becomes costly or inconvenient. Then we may discover that, ultimately, profit or survival or expediency are greater values. Or we may discover someone who would rather go out of business than produce shoddy work.

Practices

At all levels there are practices or behaviors. There are all the external manifestations which shaped and informed by beliefs, values, tradition and rituals, examples, and symbols. If the practices in your organization, or in a team, are contributing to poorly related to conflict, it is worth taking a deeper look.

A client once told me about a previous board she had worked with. Among their values these are the two: Quality and Thrift. These two values ran deep and informed their culture. However, as you may imagine, they also generated conflict. The Quality decision isn't always a Thrifty decision. Neither value is a "wrong" value. But they created friction.

It's possible that something as simple as redefining their value as "Stewardship" would have helped. Or providing a process for making a decision between quality and thrift. They hadn't really taken the time to address how to live with both.

These issues are the social equivalent of having your Check Engine light come on. This is always an unwanted experience. But it is never a wise practice to ignore it. Objective exploration leads to insight and the ability to correct underlying issues.

Culture at Work

Each workplace forms its own culture to varying degrees of strength and identity. It is easy to pick out that "Construction workers dress like/talk like…" and "Office workers dress like/talk like…" but this is focusing mostly on the Outer Layer. The inner layer has to do with professional ethics, work ethic, whether people trust each other, celebrate, or compete with each other. The core layer is the key one: This is where we discover what deep beliefs look like:

- Beliefs about abundance or scarcity: If they get theirs—will we get ours? Or we are creators of wealth and value?

- Beliefs about the value of employees: Replaceable and costly? Or family and priceless?
- Beliefs about our role with our customers: Is our role to serve them? Or to fleece them?
- Beliefs about workplace relationships: Life is about survival of the fittest? Or we can build and grow and become better people together?

These are core concepts. My bias is evident. Likely as you read through them you found yourself reacting positively or negatively to different statements. This reaction reflects your core beliefs.

The Unstoppable Force: How We Are Enculturated and What Happens When We Rely on Accidents

Like water to the fish, culture is pervasive and omnipresent in our workplaces. Unlike water to a fish, leaders have the opportunity to be shapers and crafters of their culture. New employees are formally enculturated when they attend new employee orientations. However, as anyone with job experience knows, what you are taught formally may or may not match up with what is experienced.

New employees learn to watch closely for things like:

- Exceptions to the rules: Is it possible? Who gets to and how?
- Relationships with authority: Is smiling compliance expected? Is management absent or present? Are they easily manipulated, rigid, or open to input?
- Ethics: Do our coworkers reinforce values and standards in their practices or do they support hiding and covering up?
- Innovation: Encouraged? Squelched?

Finding the Handles: Four Tools and Two Truths About How Culture Is Created, Reinforced, and Changed

The process of culture shaping is challenging. Let's explore what starts to put handles on culture so that you can steer it.

The Four Tools

1. **Strong Leadership Support:** If a leader has been in position for a while, workplace culture is nearly always a reflection of their own personal beliefs, values, and practices. As a result, if senior leadership is on board and engaged in a culture-shaping process, almost nothing can stop it. However, if leadership isn't—almost nothing short of a major crisis can change it.

2. **Consistent Communication:** Culture change can be exciting and scary. Opening lines of communication and inviting input, regular engagement, and feedback helps bring information and minimize fears and concerns.

3. **Close Alignment Between Values, Goals, and Practices:** The clearer an organization's values are as well as their goals and expectations for practices—the easier it is to train and manage them. The more aligned they are to each other (if goals are expressions values, if practices support the goals and reflect the values, and so on), the more naturally a common culture emerges.

4. **Culture is Self-Reinforcing. But Maintenance Helps:** Celebrating is one of the most powerful ways to reinforce culture. Honoring the individuals and teams who best reflect the values. Celebrating the accomplishments of others who are aligned with or are a result of your culture helps reinforce that value of what has been created.

The Two Truths

1. **There is Often Loss Before Gain:** If a culture change process is clear and thorough, some people will start to see they don't fit. They will either choose to leave or be let go. Some tools, practices, or sacred cows will no longer be congruent with the values.

2. **Culture Is Magnetic:** Like likes like. Birds of a feather flock together. Success attracts success. As your culture clarifies itself, your organization and team will naturally attract more of the kind of people who identify with your new culture. Those people will be more open to and aware of the tools and resources that better fit with this newly shaped culture.

Taming the Juggernaut: Culture Wins Every Time—So Make Friends

Culture eats strategy for lunch.

—Peter Drucker

You can ignore culture, but it doesn't ignore you. If you try to initiate a change that your organization doesn't believe in, you'll fail. If you try to get different results through using the same practices, you'll fail. If you want openness but can't handle tough feedback, you'll fail.

There are lots of ways to fail.

But there are lots of ways to win. You can't fight culture. It is self-defeating to deny it. So, you need to accept it, learn to work with it, and learn to shape it.

Conflict in culture often emerges when culture is ignored. At a visceral level, people will defend that truths they hold are self-evident. If you can speak to those cultural values and beliefs, you'll also harness their engagement, trust, and loyalty.

How to Gain Insight into Your Culture

I recently received a call from a Fortune 500 company. They have nearly 30,000 employees. The executive team and board realized that they had some cultural issues that were creating problem behaviors throughout the company. They wanted to create companywide change.

The individual reaching out to me wanted to know what kind of workshops I could offer throughout the company to help them change their culture. She also wanted to know the size of my team.

Before I answered her question, I asked, "Are these behaviors reflected on the board or executive team?" There was a pause. Then the answer, "Yes."

"Do they recognize and want to change themselves?"

"I think they are hoping that you'll work directly with the staff."

I told her it would be easier, faster, and less expensive if I worked directly with the board and executive team. In fact, if these cultural values and behaviors were held by the most senior leadership it would be futile to try to persuade change in the core values and behaviors of everyone else.

Senior leadership didn't want to change. They wanted everyone else to. They found someone else to provide an army of consultants to do workshops all over the world.

They won't experience culture change. They will experience increased frustration and dissonance organizationally.

These leaders recognized or willing to accept that they had some cultural practices that were working against their ultimate success. But they weren't willing to accept that culture was shaped by and is usually reflective of those at the top.

This is often accidental.

Just as in parenting, we influence our children, but not always in ways that we anticipate. In leadership, we shape cultures. If we don't pay attention to, and own, how we shape our cultures we remain helpless to create change.

Here's an exercise that some have found helpful. If your team culture was a religion:

- What would be the Cardinal Sins?
- What would be the Core Virtues?
- What are the Five Key Practices that everyone should do?
- What is your origin story? Why were you created and for what purpose does your organization or team exist?

Are you happy with your responses to these questions? Would your colleagues agree with your answers? What does that tell you about your culture?

CHAPTER 9

Resiliency: How to Bounce Back (Sometimes Stronger)

Earlier in my career, I became the new executive director of a financially struggling nonprofit. A mentor offered perspective that has turned out to be true, although not comforting. He observed that the nonprofits that start out easy, with all the money they need, later tend to have problems. They never learned the critical lessons offered only through struggle and hardship. It's the nonprofits that had to struggle to grow and establish themselves that often seemed healthier in the end.

This is true in business as well. Struggle creates the conditions from which wisdom and strength can emerge. Perpetual struggles, without growth, is a sign of a deeper problem. However, periodic struggles, with growth is normal and healthy. As a result, learning to struggle well is an important leadership task. This is the art of resilience.

What Is Resiliency?

Resiliency is the ability to roll with life's punches. It's the ability to bounce back from disappointment, failure, loss, conflict, and setback. It is the ability to keep doing what needs to be done when things aren't easy, the fun is gone, and the cost is rising.

As leaders, some of our opportunities of greatest impact come only during times of trouble. Understanding this makes it easier to relate to and learn in the experience of hardship. This is most particularly true when the hardship is a conflict.

One thing I love most about the entrepreneurial community is that it is a community of resilience. Perseverance. Pioneering. They are familiar with struggling. They've experienced loss and success. They have the scars and stories to prove it.

Better than that, they enjoy the rewards of having overcome. Successful businesses. High impact nonprofits. Rewarding relationships at home and at work.

Resiliency in Conflict Is Critical

Resiliency is crucially important when it comes to addressing workplace conflict. Conflict can be difficult to resolve. However, the most difficult aspect of it is the willingness to try. When people are willing to try, especially if they are willing to try something different, conflicts nearly always resolve between two willing parties.

There are two keys: (1) willingness and (2) tolerance for discomfort.

Some people are willing. But only as long as they aren't challenged, don't have to face uncomfortable emotions or truths, don't have to address consequences. Or they are willing as long as they can do it their way (which isn't true willingness)?

Others are willing to be extraordinarily uncomfortable, in terms of putting up with poor behavior and the costs of unaddressed issues. Like the apocryphal frog in boiling water they'd rather ignore the small accumulation of problems. But they aren't willing to address the issue until it is too late.

You need both.

Nearly everyone you know and work with addresses conflict poorly. It's possible that you do as well. Much, if not most, of what makes us unwilling or intolerant of discomfort is the *perception* of what will happen. The fear or anxiety around an encounter. The unsubstantiated beliefs of what the other person has or will said or do. The catastrophizing of the event.

It's difficult.

In most cases, while the substantive elements of a conflict may have some complexity, the largest issues are emotional and personal. And much of that is perceived. Not objective.

As a result, it takes courage, intent, and practice to learn to relate to conflict more effectively. It takes trial and error. A willingness to be the *bigger person* when you feel you've been wronged or are misunderstood.

Leaders can make this significantly easier for everyone else by modeling the way. As leaders demonstrate that conflicts happen, that there are appropriate ways to address poor behavior, unmet expectations, violated values, possible misunderstandings, and so on—it makes it easier for everyone else.

To do this, leaders must begin with their own relationship with conflict.

All Conflict Is Physical: How Our Body and Brain Responds to Conflict

Most conflicts, for most people, are physical events. Even when the conflict is healthy and appropriate. Most people know this intuitively. In fact, many people won't believe there is a conflict unless they can see or hear physical signs of it such as a raised voice, a red face, or a fist thumping on a table. The truth is that most of the time conflict isn't visible or audible. People are far more likely to try to avoid it, quietly, with a smile on their face than let anyone know they are bothered.

However, I'm talking about a deeper physiology. What happens to us, internally, when we perceive a threat to our significance, to our safety, or to our sense of satisfaction.

What happens is observable through changes in our hormone levels and through neural imagery (Gottman 1999, McEwen and Morrison 2017), we see that our brains shift into survival mode. Fight or flight. Or sometimes we freeze.

This is the physical side of the stress reaction. We experience stress when we perceive to have been harmed. Or when we believe we *may* be harmed.

In the face of harm (real or perceived) our brains release stress hormones, such as adrenaline, epinephrine, and cortisol. These hormones position us for survival.

When we believe we will be harmed, our brain will respond similarly as if we've experienced actual harm. Our brains do a poor job of differentiating between what we imagine and what we experience. For example, anticipating someone's negative response toward us in an upcoming meeting, or that a presentation will be poorly received. This will trigger a stress response that is nearly the same as if we actually experienced the event. Our brain doesn't distinguish well between what we imagine and what we experience.

Our brain doesn't release one set of hormones when you realize you have a conflict with a coworker and different when being chased by a bear.

It's the same set of hormones.

Not only do we experience these hormones, but the person we are dealing with is likely experiencing them as well.

These hormones are valuable. And they are powerful. They motivate us to act. They help us stay focused and awake. They impact our metabolism, they are anti-inflammatory, they impact our short-term memory and blood pressure. Even the salt and water levels in our body are impacted.

It's a major physical event.

In fact, the impact of these hormones is so strong, that chronic and intense conflict during pregnancy can impact the in-utero development of a child's brain and body.

At a healthy level, with a healthy sense of challenge, we are more focused, able to think and move faster, and respond more efficiently.

At a spiked level, we are still able to act quickly but it is more reactive. When confronted by a bear, this might be lifesaving. Contemplation, scenarios planning, and pros and cons lists would get us killed.

When in conflict, we tend to revert to our conditioning. Unfortunately, most of our conditioning is helpful only for survival. Survival is not always the same thing as building healthy, trusting, and collaborative relationships.

At a visceral level, most of us believe that conflict is dangerous. We need to overcome it or avoid it. So, we yell, deny, avoid, manipulate, blame, attack, threaten, posture, and so on.

Not because we planned to start yelling, or to storm out of the room slamming the door, or shut down and go blank. But because we lost control and didn't have another set of options or habits that were easily accessible through the hormonal cloud.

In a normal marriage conflict (excluding scenarios of domestic abuse), survival is a lousy goal. It's almost axiomatic that if you've won an argument in a marriage, you've lost. Unless it is a playful discussion,

I can't *win* against my wife. And even when kidding around, it's best to be careful!

It is a very similar dynamic in the workplace. In disagreements about personal respect, workplace safety, budget priorities, or deployment of resources—survival is possible. But it's tough to say that survival creates a genuine *win* in the big picture.

This is why the military, emergency services professionals and combat athletes train repetitively. So, when confronted with high levels of stress, their conditioning and muscle memory kick in. This allows individuals and teams to not only survive but also continue to safely move forward toward their objectives.

As I've mentioned, I practice Brazilian Jiu-Jitsu. A combat sport. I definitely want to survive. It's no fun getting smashed into the mat or choked out. Even more, I want to win a match.

Where I train, every class has a segment of sparring or "rolling" as we call it. On my very first day of training, my first match was with the head instructor. I didn't know anything. I had no idea what to do and here I was matched with a black belt. So, I asked him what I should do. "Do whatever makes sense to you," he said.

So, I freaked out.

I went nuts and fought as hard as I could. I found out later that this is a fairly typical "newbie" thing to do. It was also why the head instructor matched himself with me.

He wasn't going to freak out in return. He had the skills and confidence to keep both of us safe. He's smaller than me but I was suddenly reminded of wrestling with my dad as a young child. In fact, he just kind of surfed on top of me. He used his own response to me to teach me one of the most important lessons of Brazilian Jiu Jitsu: *Stay calm.*

That was not an easy lesson for me. In fact, it took me several months to learn how to stay calm. I learned it by rolling with more experienced grapplers who consistently, calmly beat me.

Regular training, practice, and conditioning teaches me how to instinctively pursue goals larger than survival and winning. Those goals include avoiding personal harm, avoiding causing harm to a training partner, managing my emotions, moderating my efforts if someone is smaller or less experienced than I, and helping myself or others pursue a training goal that may not result in my winning a match.

In the world of Brazilian Jiu-Jitsu, this all takes places with regular training in a 100 percent effort, full-contact martial art.

If all I did was fight to survive or win, I would lose willing training partners. I would get hurt. It would be a slow road to learn and improve.

Working With Our Bodies

It's not important that you remember which stress hormones do what exactly. It is helpful to know that when in conflict and you start to feel sick in your stomach, or an adrenaline buzz, or heightened blood pressure, or whatever it is you experience, your brain is gearing you up to be reactive. Not to be objective and rational. It isn't preparing you to be respectful, curious, or caring toward others.

It is also helpful to know that this experience is shared by others.

Which is why conflict gets so weird, so quickly.

But There Are Practical Things You Can Do

1. **Calm yourself.** John Gottman, a leading researcher and psychologist focusing on marriage and relationships conducted an experiment (Gottman 1999). His findings translate to the workplace.

   He brought together couples and got them to argue about something. Once the argument had escalated, they let the control group continue to argue it out. With a sample group, they intervened and separated them for 20-minute cool down period. Then they brought them back together and let them continue their argument.

   They discovered that the control group, the group with no cool down period, had a low percentage of success in arriving at a resolution. The sample group, however, improved both their ability to arrive at resolution as well as shortened the time frame to get there.

   What they found was that the hormonal flooding that took place in an escalated conflict inhibited successful resolution. It takes about 20 minutes for your body to flush adrenaline from the system. The 20-minute break allowed for this flushing to happen. The couples who had this opportunity, enjoyed a higher percentage of success at achieving resolution.

Practical ideas:

- **Call a break if needed.** It helps to frame this without blaming the other person for needing the break. For example, "I'm not responding to this conversation in the way that I would like. I'd like to take a minute to think about what we are talking about and my response. Can we take a break and reconnect in 20 minutes?" (Or whenever is appropriate.)

   The key elements of this question are: (1) personal ownership—no blame shifting, (2) not running away from the conversation but naming a specific time to reconnect.

   When on that break: The following have proven to be helpful for many people. They can all be done simultaneously, but even just using one of these will be helpful:

- **If available, take a walk.** Research has demonstrated that walking around greenery has a stronger benefit in reducing stress. However, any walking will be helpful as long as you are walking somewhere safe that doesn't require being alert. The physical movement also can help your system flush the stress hormones.

- **Deep, slow breathing.** When stressed, many people start to breathe shallow breathes from the top of their lungs. These deplete the body of oxygen. Deep breathing helps you replenish your oxygen, which aids with hormonal flushing. Additionally, by deep breathing, the movement of your diaphragm manipulates your vagus nerve. This has the impact of mechanically slowing your heart rate down. Which helps you physically calm yourself.

- **Practice gratitude.** One of the fastest ways I've found to turn my own attitude around is to practice gratitude. I will force myself to think through a list of 10 things I'm grateful for about this person or situation. So far, I've never gotten to the end of that list without shifting to a much better place emotionally and mentally.

- **Get clear about what you want from this conversation:** Think through The Four Steps to Resolution. This process is helpful to many people. It'll help you map a path through the confusion of the conflict and help create clarity about what is wanted in terms of outcomes and relationship.

- **Positive visualization.** Most people struggle with intentionally visualizing. However, we all slip into unintentional visualizations regularly. These typically take the form of fantasy. This might feel positive such as something we like: an upcoming vacation, what we'll do with a bonus, or connecting with someone we're attracted to. Or they might be negative: imagining an argument, imagining a confrontation, thinking through how we'll avoid, or outwit an argument. Either way, we all do this unintentionally.

  You can be intentional about this. Instead of imagining how we'll defeat an argument or get our jabs in, use that ability to imagine a positive outcome. Imagining it won't make it happen, of course. But it does increase the likelihood of a positive outcome. It's very difficult to achieve a positive outcome that we can't imagine. You are primarily relying on the other person to think of something on your behalf or trusting in a lucky accident.

When you take your break, don't ruminate on the blow-by-blow. Focus on the future you want to create. This is leadership.

2. **Calm Your People**

    If the conflict is within a team or group, leaders will benefit from *use of self.* As you stay calm (or regain a calm state) you'll find that others will be assured and influenced by you. Additionally, the following can be helpful:

    - **Framing/Reframing:** Just like a picture frame can significantly impact the look of a painting or photograph, the frame around an issue impacts how and what others see in it. If it is an emerging issue, it can be very helpful for a leader to frame it in objective and optimistic terms. Additionally, it is very helpful to frame issues in terms of questions. The questions focus people's attention.

For example, in the context of budget cuts: *I want to assure everyone that your jobs are secure. We need to make some short-term adjustments so that, in the long term, we can get back on step.* In a conflict about budgets, which can become symbolic for "which of us has the most important project" which we interpret as, "Which of us is the most valued person," hormonally, we just see bears. The questions we need to answer are: What short term adjustments are needed? How do we limit the negative impact that these adjustments might make on staff?

Reframing is also powerful. If a conflict or issue has existed for even a short amount of time, it starts to get a name and a negative framing. "The warehouse issue." "The grow no matter what" faction. "The good old boy club." It is a critical leadership opportunity to step in, and reframe the issue in objective, noninflammatory terms that allow everyone to focus together.

Example: *"This issue isn't really about the warehouse crew or the retail crew, we're really looking at a communication system that hasn't grown along with the company. How do we improve and standardize communication between retail locations and the warehouse?"*

3. Practice

Practice being in healthy conflict. I'll talk more about this later in the chapter. The point here is to create regular opportunities for healthy conflict to emerge, to not only work on having those conversations but also be able to evaluate the quality of the conversation.

If there is low trust on the team, or if individuals are highly conflict adverse, start with very simple or low consequence issues.

One way to do this is to require each team member to communicate one strength and one weakness of an idea before making a decision on it. This may seem like it could be time consuming, but it'll usually save time and improve idea selection and implementation because there will be less ongoing conflict and more buy-in.

If you are on an aggressive team (or a team where there are aggressive individuals) setting and enforcing ground rules that require respectful behavior, encourage the input from everyone, and slow down the pace of conversation. These ground rules should help improve the process of your conversation. You can draw these out of the group. Common ones include:

- Treat each other with respect
- No interrupting
- Everyone will participate in the conversation
- We will be on time
- No texting, browsing, or phones

4. **Change the Norms—By Focusing on Behaviors**
   This is about creating a place that feels safe for people to disagree in. It takes time for many groups to learn that it is safe. It may take time for new members to learn this. Psychological safety in conflict usually requires consistent behaviors that reinforce the following:
   - **Significance**: Remembering to value the individual even if there is a disagreement about a decision, opinion, or behavior. Leaders who model respectful language, volume, tones, and approaches help tremendously. People will tend to match a leader's tone.
   - **Safety:** Once in a while I work with groups who have experienced physical threats or fights. More often there is the fear of retribution. One of the great challenges in a conflict is that it can become very unsafe to communicate half-baked ideas or not fully thought through sentiments. The rawness and incompleteness of this often creates friction.

     In the legal and mediation professions these dynamic conversations (negotiations) can be legally protected. In part, this is so that there is space to try out ideas without the concern that someone will publicize them. Experience has shown that first impressions, positions, emotions, or ideas are rarely where things land. Creating space for them to be brought out into the open and discussed helps.

Ensure that no one will be penalized for speaking up or having different opinions. Sometimes the penalization is informal: avoidance of eye contact, a noninvitation to lunch, and so on. As a leader, being sure to seek out, validate, and include people who expressed an unpopular opinion helps restore them to the group.

- **Satisfaction:** The immediate pursuit of *The Good Life* often feels like it takes a detour when there is conflict. However, by reasonably accommodating schedules, or interests, you can help diminish resistance. Often time, the behavior of listening well can help defuse someone's frustration.

Building Blocks of Resiliency

Relationships

Research demonstrates that people with a strong support system are able to manage challenges more easily. Because of this, leaders who are married or have families should invest the time to build and maintain healthy marriages and families. They'll function better at work.

Leaders who build strong friendships as well as peer and mentoring relationships create strength for themselves. They aren't easily knocked off track. If they are, they can get back on track faster.

Since most people choose marriage or having a family: It's not that just getting married or having a family automatically makes you resilient. It's the process of *building* healthy relationships at home that contributes to your resilience at work. Your home life is an environment rich with opportunities to learn to relate to conflict differently. The closeness or proximity of family creates a unique environment not easily replicated in normal friendships or social relationships. This is one reason why it is important not to create an "either/or" relationship between family and work. Learning to be healthy in one can contribute to the health of the other.

I'm not suggesting that marriage and family is "the thing" you need to do. I didn't marry until my mid-thirties. Previous to that, I found that it was important avoid my tendency to create a domestic life where I didn't have to deal with issues (often my own) that I didn't want to deal with. So, I intentionally had roommates and involved myself on boards or teams where there was a need to learn to build and maintain relationships.

Additionally, cultivating relationships with people who care about you, are encouraging, motivated and positive also strengthens your support system. They might be friends, peers, or mentors. Avoid spending discretionary time with people who drain you. Limit time with people who primarily complain, blame others, or lack motivation. They don't handle adversity well themselves.

Build close and committed relationships with healthy people. Both the process of learning to build the relationship and just having the relationships will contribute to your personal growth and resiliency.

Efficacy

Cultivate a sense of *can do*. The best leaders act and know why they are acting. Cultivating this sense of *can do* is primarily done by actively focusing on what *you* can do in a given situation. This is opposed to focusing on the things that are done to you.

Many people tend to view life through the lens that they are victims or helpless. There is always something out there that prevents them from acting. *"The Man is getting me down"* or, *"You can't beat the system,"* or *"Those people..."* are always preventing success or satisfaction. *Can do* leaders recognize that while there may be others who offer resistance— their focus is on what they can do to create the results they want. As a result, they steadily expand their experience, ability, and influence.

Appreciation

Become a "good finder" as Zig Ziglar used to say. Actively cultivating a habit of gratitude is one of the most powerful and life changing steps you'll ever take. Closely related to this, learning to see value in and communicate appreciation to others is one of the simplest yet powerful attitudes of a leader.

I used to struggle deeply with cynicism and being judgmental. I still lean toward perfectionism. I won't say that I've completely overcome those tendencies. But I will say I'm gaining significant ground. I've changed dramatically since I began to actively practice good finding.

Being able to look for and find good when you are facing a challenge or disappointment is absolutely fundamental to your ability to be resilient.

Vision

Remember what you are pursuing and *why*. Going through hardship for the sake of hardship is silly. A clear vision of what you are trying to create or protect is critical. Regularly reminding yourself of why you are enduring a challenge provides fuel and focus. It creates meaning and direction when you are tempted to feel helpless or hopeless.

Attitude of Growth

A mentor of mine, Alan Weiss, frequently says: *If you can grow 1% each day, in 70 days you'll be twice as good.* What he is encouraging is two things: (1) Look for growth opportunities every day and (2) Pursue consistent incremental growth.

Viewing challenges as opportunities to grow and learn shifts them from being all negative experiences to experiences where growth is possible. On a personal level shifting from trying to avoid or survive challenges to intentionally trying to find the lessons made available by them. On a corporate level, I observe how my best clients actively pursue growth even in a down or scared economy. They see the realities of the environment and venture into it assuming they'll grow and become stronger as a result.

Along with this, view challenges as opportunities to experiment with new attitudes or approaches. Too often challenge puts us into reactive mode. Taking an active stance and exploring how this situation might be tackled, related to, or perceived differently allows for growth.

Using Conflict to Create Resiliency in Teams

For a leader, a team conflict is a wonderful moment. It offers a rich opportunity.

Let me illustrate this by offering a contrast. I recently took my Toyota 4 Runner in for a routine oil change. When I received it back, they let me know that a part was failing and it needed to be replaced.

That's never desired news. I've never looked forward to repairs.

In part, this is because once the vehicle is repaired, it is still only back to normal. It is repaired. Not improved. I feel like I'm inconvenienced to get back to what I thought I already had.

While it is technically possible to improve some elements of my vehicle when I repair it, for most people, most of the time the goal is to regain the status quo.

With people, with teams, this can and should be different. I would suggest that it may even be a failure of leadership to take the opportunity of conflict and only attempt to restore the status quo. In teams, conflict is an opportunity to build an even stronger team. It's a diagnostic test of what works and what doesn't.

To try to wring what I can out of the car analogy, it is less like bringing in a vehicle to be repaired and more like being able to upgrade it to next year's model (which is hopefully an improvement). Except it's the same car.

As I've mentioned before, conflict is where deep values, interests, or desires begin to surface. It is where we begin to see which mindsets, behaviors, and attitudes best serve the team and which don't. It is where we can see how the systems or processes or structures support what we are trying to accomplish and experience and when they don't.

In a healthy conflict, the leader is very alert to all of these possibilities. In the healthiest of conflicts, so are the members of the teams. When there is a denied project, an offensive comment, a misunderstanding, or repeated poor performance, there is—right with it—an opportunity to answer the following questions:

- **Are we safe?** Do we trust each other? Do we care about each other? If not, are we willing to create safety for others?
- **Will we try?** Will we pull together and work through difficult conversations? Will we be willing to make changes to our systems or culture? Or will we quit, fight, or run?

The capacity for resiliency on a team is largely set by the leader's answers to those questions for the team as a whole *and* for the individuals.

Let's explore these questions:

Are We Safe?

There are two sides to this question. The first is "Are we relationally and psychologically safe right now?" Most people's personal stories have told them the answer to this question is "No." Conflict, all conflict, is viewed as a threat. It means something that is desired may not be attained or may be taken away. It means the end of something: A relationship, a good time or an opportunity.

This does not create a sense of safety. One of my best clients has an executive team that does conflict well. They confront, they argue, there are emotions, and there is honesty. They also respect each and value each other. They pursue the success of each other.

While they may initially feel threatened in the immediate conflict, they have learned, "This will work out. I will be heard. We will grow." The safety exists in this group primarily because the company owner possesses an admirable combination of assertiveness, ambition, personal humility, and genuine care for others. He addresses issues. He puts stuff out there. He isn't always right, but he isn't timid. He expects his team to engage him.

I've watched many leaders attempt to do this. Many miss it because they require their team to out-argue them. They turn situations into a match of wits. This won't feel safe to many people.

My client appropriately wants solid rationale, but is also willing to listen for or through a poorly articulated statement.

His ego is real. It gets in the way. But it is also resilient. He doesn't require that his team beat him in an argument. He doesn't have to win or be beat. He remembers this isn't a contest.

I love working with them. Over the last six years they have become one of the most successful companies in their industry, performing in the top one percent nationally. Their capacity for addressing conflict is a crucial part of what makes this possible.

They argue as a team. Not competitors.

The second part of answering this question of safety is "Will we address and confront unsafe people/behaviors?" It is very common for leaders to avoid confrontation with people who aren't safe for the others on the team. Reasons I often hear are: "She is going through a really difficult time right now." Or "He has been with us since the beginning."

Or "He's got a few rough edges but is really great at…." Or, the most common, "I don't know how to replace her."

This can also be extended to unsafe policies or working environments.

If a leader allows unsafe people or situations to continue to damage and hurt others without decisively addressing them, the leader loses credibility.

The people with options, who are often the best and the healthiest staff, will leave. The rest will often learn to shut down, not speak up, and avoid certain situations or responsibilities.

In some circumstances, if there is a fairly resilient team in place *and* mechanisms that make it possible, the team may force the leader out. But this is rare.

The leader sets the tone for and demonstrates how to be resilient.

If the answer to this question of safety is "No," it becomes very difficult for resolution or growth to occur. However, it is still possible if the answer to the next question is a, "Yes."

Will We Try?

When qualifying possible mediation clients, I look for people's willingness to engage in good faith. Are they willing to at least try? Are they willing to follow through on their commitments?

If they are willing, 95 percent of my clients find a resolution.

Now, resolution may not look like, "We're all going to continue this same path together." But it does meet the modest standard of a mutually acceptable path forward.

If any of the parties are unwilling to try, nothing will change. I don't take the contract or will cancel it. Willingness is that important.

Again, the leader sets the tone for this. A leader who demonstrates an authentic effort to improve a situation, even if imperfectly, will find that they have increased the likelihood that others will try as well.

As a leader does try, and a team does work through a conflict well, they develop a new story or history with each other. Regardless of their personal stories, they start to learn that, "Here, in this place, it's safe and people will work with each other to understand each other."

This helps create a culture where healthy conflict happens.

Tools for Building Resiliency

1. **Gratitude and Positivity/Appreciation:** Make a list of three things that you are grateful for. Think of someone close to you and identify one thing you appreciate about them. Tell them this one thing. Keep it short. A text or e-mail works just as well. Try these two simple habits (gratitude and appreciation) for 21 days. Let me know how it shifted your ability to be a "good finder." It will.

2. **Building Relationships:** Think of one person who encourages and motivates you. List three ways you can spend more time with this person. Is there anyone else you'd like to add to this list?

3. **Efficacy:** Think about what you need to accomplish today or this week. Create two lists: (1) what concerns me, and (2) what I can control. Aim to have at least 10 items on each list. What are two items of concern (that you can't control) that you can choose to stop focusing on? What are two items of control that you can accomplish?

4. **Vision:** What is the ideal state that you are trying to create in your team and work life? Write it out. Describe it as clearly as you can. You can only build what you are able to see. Keep this vision with you and review it on a regular basis.

5. **Attitude of Growth:** Journaling is helpful for many. It is a convenient place to explore what we might be learning in the moment. It is also a great place to review and record lessons from recent experiences. I've found that by doing personal debriefs with myself, I've been able to capture lessons from experiences more quickly. Think of a challenge you are facing or recently faced. What are two or three things you've learned (or can learn) from that experience? The next time you face a similar situation what will you do the same? What will you do differently? In what way?

CHAPTER 10

Healthy Tension: What It Really Is, How to Practice It

The word *conflict* connotes all kinds of imagery and emotions for people. Nearly all of which tend to be negative.

Sometimes it's worth the battle to try to expand or change the definition of a word. I've been doing that for most of this book: helping the reader begin to view conflict as a leadership opportunity. Conflict is something we do. We mostly have not done it well. However, we can do it well. Actually, we can be great at it.

Sometimes it's just easier to use a different word. It avoids some of the negative connotations. If, when working with your team, you find it is taking too much effort to help them emotionally accept the word conflict as a neutral word—but an experience that can be negatively or productively addressed—let me recommend another term: Healthy Tension.

I hope I've already answered why we want it: It is an important opportunity to understand what is really important to people, to improve relationships, to engineer more effective systems, and to develop a more vibrant culture.

Cultivating Curiosity

Any new practitioner of Brazilian Jiu-Jitsu shares a common experience. There is a very early, and often lengthy plateau where nothing you learn makes sense and you spend all your time getting crushed, beat up, smothered, and tied into knots. This is so common that when a new practitioner starts to express their confusion and frustration, everyone else will start nodding and sharing their own stories.

The only way to get through it is to go through it. The good news? Everyone who perseveres gets through it. It isn't a question of talent, fitness, aptitude, or anything else. It's just perseverance. To have that level of perseverance, it really helps to stay interested in the sport. To stay curious.

Dr. Todd Kashdan, a researcher at George Mason University, has found that individuals with higher levels of curiosity also experience higher levels of life satisfaction (Kashdan and Roberts 2004).

One explanation for this is that greater curiosity propels people past the initial discomfort of the unfamiliar or learning phase into a phase where they can reap the benefits of what they've learned.

To develop a capacity for healthy tension, a leader needs to build personal curiosity as well as a culture of curiosity.

Curiosity, or a genuine interest in, "What's going on here?" suggests a level of suspended judgment, humility, and a willingness to explore which is valuable both for invention and exploration as well as conflict resolution.

Children start out asking hundreds of questions a day. Not all of them are curiosity based. Many are asking for something. But even those start with the assumption that an unknown answer will likely be positive.

Over time, children and then adults ask fewer and fewer questions. Some of this is just efficiency. We have learned more about the facts of daily life. We've also developed constructs of "how things work" which help us navigate decisions without needing to spend a lot of time researching or thinking about it. There is value in both.

However, we may have just stopped caring. We may have become satisfied with the puddles we play in and lose interest in the ocean nearby.

Tragically, we also learn that certain questions are perceived to be a waste of time, stupid, provoke defensiveness, impatience or frustration, will only be answered by, "No," or make you look weak or unknowledgeable. We learn to stop being curious.

This happens individually and culturally.

Curiosity Killers

In general, the following are the top killers of curiosity within a team culture. As a leader, *modeling* the desired behavior is the most powerful tool at your disposal. Along with demonstrating *how* to be curious, you give permission to slow down and explore.

Black and White Thinking

For many people, there is a very common tendency to utilize only two boxes for sorting all information. We might label those boxes as Right/Wrong, I Like/I Don't Like, Familiar/Unfamiliar, or Win/Lose. Of course, they don't think about these labels. We might just feel a strong disagreement, fear, or discomfort.

One of the great challenges of this kind of thinking is it is often fueled by the experience or understanding that being wrong is so completely wrong. It often isn't just a question of being mistaken in judgment, but the perception of being, somehow, wrong as a person.

It's for that reason that it isn't helpful to tell someone they are wrong for black and white thinking.

It also isn't helpful to suggest that there are shades of gray. This feels like pushing someone to accept moral or personal compromise. They'll most of often resist this.

For people who have black or white tendencies, the most effective way to demonstrate curiosity is to practice being curious. To ask good questions, be a good listener to the individual or the group. To suspend judgment. To avoiding shaming and practice preserving the dignity of others. To avoid zero-sum scenarios and look for mutual wins.

As we model this, others start to see that more options are possible.

Scarcity Stress

Many people stop being curious just because they are so stressed for resources (money, time, emotional margin, health, etc.). As mentioned earlier, stress reactions push people to act quickly. If you are being chased by a bear, it's the wrong time to pull out a white board and start brainstorming solutions. Stress forces a decision. Although, not always the best decision.

There are many sources of stress that limit workplace creativity. One is poor or incomplete information. Another is scarcity (real or perceived) of finances and time.

As a leader, working to remove or mitigate inaccurate or incomplete information can be helpful. It can also be helpful to explore artificial scarcity. Timelines and budgets can often be adjusted.

Imagine a situation of real scarcity: For example, a real economic downturn with significant market changes. A company is in debt and may go bankrupt within the next year unless changes are made. Conflict is very common as cuts may be needed and jobs go on the line.

It's in this scenario that real leadership is needed: to remind the team of their assets and abilities. Speak to past challenges that have been overcome, to the strengths on the team, to opportunities on the horizon, the short-term wins that can be pursued, to a vision that includes overcoming the current challenge.

As a leader, you need to provide the emotional space so that others can begin to think differently. It means making sure that you are able to separate or bracket your own concerns and develop a compelling picture of the future.

Accustomed to Authoritarianism

Many workplaces have learned that "He is the boss." Or "She asks for your opinion but does whatever she wants anyway." Over time two things happen: (1) People stop being curious and wait to be told what to do. They learn that curiosity and exploration may not be encouraged or even tolerated. They stop practicing and lose the ability to think creatively or critically. Instead they learn how to take orders or hold on to their little bit of turf. (2) The most creative and emotionally confident people will likely leave. So, you'll end up with a workforce of people who prefer to be told what to do and avoid responsibility and decision making. While this may seem onerous on its face, the reality is many people prefer the simplicity of not having to do the work or carry responsibility for decision-making.

This is not the kind of thinking that solves problems or builds vibrant workplaces.

Lack of Process

In most cases, decisions do need to be made. Curiosity and exploration need limits. Processes that guide this make it easier for people to engage.

Many workplaces have had the experience of brainstorming processes that went nowhere, never seemed to end, or only open up various cans of worms. As a result, they are wary of the value of brainstorming or curiosity. An effective process should provide structure to the conversation, describe how people are included, and how a decision will be arrived.

Many managers or leaders have learned one or two facilitation tools and that's it. Often, one of them may be *Robert's Rules of Order*. This process is complicated, few people understand it, and many are intimidated by it. While it has definite value in the right time and place, it requires both.

Whenever I offer the services of mediation or facilitation, I spend time identifying the most appropriate process for the conversation. A conversation between a divorcing husband and wife who own and operate a business together requires a different process than working with a board in conflict with their CEO which requires different process than addressing and engaging hundreds of stakeholders.

Many processes for working with smaller teams are relatively simple and can be learned quickly. However, there is high value in bringing in a skilled professional to either coach the leader to learn and utilize a new process or to provide the services directly.

Ambiguity Discomfort

Many people, often many leaders, are uncomfortable with ambiguity. They have an emotional need for closure. Staying undecided on issues doesn't feel good. Let's figure it out and move on.

On a number of occasions, I've worked with groups of attorneys and judges who were forming or changing organizations. In each occasion, there was a strong tendency to try to button down the legal documents for the organizations and put up marketing material. When I asked them strategic questions related to, "Why are you creating this?" or "What do you hope to accomplish?" there was resistance regarding entering into a deliberative process. In each case, they would shift to the tactical actions of creating bylaws, reviewing policies, or putting up websites (usually with no content on them).

They had a strong discomfort around ambiguity. It was strong enough that they avoided questions that didn't have clear right or wrong answers and instead just required decent decision making.

But this isn't only legal professionals. Many executives are good at making fast decisions. They struggle when it is more helpful to slow down and maintain a state of curiosity for a time.

Cultivating Courage

Courage is the first of human qualities because it is the quality which guarantees the others.

—Aristotle

Courage is what it takes to stand up and speak; courage is also what it takes to sit down and listen.

—Winston Churchill

Fear. Courage.

Fear isn't the opposite of courage. Instead, fear is the context within which courage can occur and has meaning.

While we don't often use words like *fear* or *courage* in leadership, they exist and often dominate the thinking. On a regular basis, leaders (whether individually or as a team) need to lead into the unknown.

Often, the greatest unknowns have boundaries well demarcated by lines of fear. Often, the knowns are equally surrounded by fear.

When I provide executive coaching I often begin with a 360-degree assessment process for a leader. Most leaders are nervous, or feel some level of fear, regarding the results. In fact, some will actually try to avoid doing it altogether or will opt out of working with me because this is part of my process.

I've always found this interesting. It's not as if we're going to discover anything that doesn't already exist. We aren't creating opinions or perspectives about the leader. We're just bringing them out into the open so they can be related to directly.

I *do* understand that it can be intimidating to hear what people truly think about us. We're often afraid of what they'll say. It takes courage to ask.

Fear.

Too many leaders *don't* have certain conversations because of concerns of what might happen if that topic is brought up.

Too often, leaders *don't* implement certain decisions because of fear of how people will respond—although it is very common that people are waiting for them to act on those decisions.

Too frequently, leaders *avoid* dealing with issues, hoping they'll go away on their own.

It is insufficiently accurate, but often quoted advice, "It's best to avoid stirring things up." While it is true that if you don't know how to deal with the issue, it might be better not to poke around in it. But that doesn't mean the issue shouldn't be dealt with. The right answer is to learn how to deal with it or get help. To just let issues sit is negligence.

Here is what I find helps with building courage:

Getting Help (It's Better with a Friend!)

As a team, learn to *en-courage* (put courage into) each other. As a leader, surround yourself with people (friends, mentors, coaches) who have courage and handle the kinds of situations you are facing. Don't face them alone. Get help.

Getting Information (Let's Shed Some Light on the Situation!)

In my experience, most fear is based on a lack of information or misinformation. Basically, we are mostly afraid of the stories that we create to fill in the blanks. For some reason we fill in those blanks with monsters more frequently than butterflies.

One of the truly great values of planning processes is not so much the end-product of the plan. It is the fact that we've been able to make a thought experiment out of the future, where we take a step-by-step journey and make sure that everyone feels reasonably safe along the way. This is one of the reasons why discussing how to implement a plan should be a part of any responsible planning process.

In workplace conflicts, there is a dramatic amount of unknown information about what other people are thinking, what they actually did or said, what was intended or about consequences. But there is a lot of fear. Fear often manifested as anger or frustration or avoidance. Getting sound and current data, all on its own, is one of the most powerful ways to dispel fear and mitigate conflict.

Easy Wins (David Didn't Start With Goliath)

Develop experience being courageous, start with small wins. David's first challenge wasn't Goliath. The Biblical story of David never tells us what his first challenge was. But it does describe him as being a shepherd. Often the work of boys. It may be that he spent a lot of time out on his own. He might have gotten lost, he might have gotten lonely, he might have been scared of the dark. All of which he learned he could face and overcome regardless of how he felt about it. At some point, he even learned to protect his sheep when lions or bears attacked.

He faced the giant Goliath after building a personal inventory of facing and overcoming smaller challenges.

Regularly take on small challenges. Or break the big challenge down into a series of small challenges. When I coach leaders, I often set up situations where they regularly tackle small challenges. When they get in the habit of doing this regularly they establish a track record of success. Their self-confidence or courage grows dramatically and quickly.

Accountability (Get It in the Open)

Sometimes a coach helps create accountability. Sometimes your team can. When I first decided I wanted to write a book, it was intimidating. So, I announced I was going to do this to my newsletter list. Public accountability. It helped motivate me to do something that I felt uncertain about.

Changing behavior is hard. Addictive behaviors, even more difficult. Support groups like Alcoholics Anonymous have the success record they do because they provide and encourage living openly and staying accountable.

Leaders who want to grow quickly, find opportunities for accountability. They find mentors, they hire coaches, and they join mastermind groups. Finding people to walk with you and challenge you regarding behaviors and results helps you build courage.

Learning Skills

My oldest son is five. He loves being in the water. However, he's never been particularly confident in the water on his own. He has tended to be very clingy, which makes sense. He didn't know how to swim.

When he recently took swim lessons his confidence shot through the roof. Next thing I knew he went from clinging tightly to me to running to jump into the deep end of the pool! That was overconfidence…and a demonstration of why it was valuable that he had others around him to fish him back out of the water! But his courage wasn't dampened.

Learning skills helped him gain that courage. I've found that many leaders want to operate safely within their strengths and where their skills are comfortable, which means unless their strengths and skills expand, their leadership will always be limited.

Leaders who constantly cultivate their skills, honing existing skills and developing new ones, will often find that new challenges or the unknown don't hold the same level of intimidation.

Self-Awareness and Ownership

I recently worked with a client, a first-time entrepreneur. She's creative, motivated, has great ideas, and is willing to grow and make changes. One of the issues she wanted to talk about was team dynamics. "My @#%$@ team is driving me crazy!" "They aren't supportive!" "They are always negative!" She had a string of strongly worded complaints about various people on her team. She also regularly communicated doubt that success was possible (even though she's in a great position to do very well).

I asked if she talked this way to her team. "Oh yes, we don't keep anything from each other."

I explained to her that, as leader, she's the shaper of her company's story. She influences everyone else's narrative or perspective of what is. She might feel moments of doubt or frustration or insecurity, but she needs to be careful to bracket those. In other words, she can feel them, but she should find appropriate places, times, and people to communicate them to. Her employees need to hear that she sees success, answers, solutions, and is willing to make the decisions and changes to achieve them.

Many people live without a strong awareness of what they are feeling, how they express themselves, or why they are reacting the way they are. As leaders, these same people aren't aware of how they impact others.

In the fields of emotional and relational intelligence, the ability to be aware of one's own self is a powerful starting point for learning how to relate more effectively with others. In the study of leadership 360 surveys, the leaders whose self-assessment most closely aligns with the assessments of others tend to be the most effective (even when they recognize a weakness).

As a consultant, my use of self is one of the most important tools that I have. My personality, my energy levels, my sense of humor, the way I look, my emotional state, and my confidence all work together to create a sense of *presence*. As a consultant, I have to stay aware of my current state *and for the benefit of my clients* determine how to best show up to serve them.

I'm not a chameleon. I'm always very much me. But I have to own my feelings, my mindsets, how I look and determine how all of this can best serve my client.

Learning to Listen

I think I'm good in tense conversations precisely because my tendency is to be poor at them.

I naturally want to do many of the things that don't work: get my thoughts in, win the conversation, make judgments about the other person, get bored, start thinking about what I want to say and so on.

I have a lot of experience of none of that being helpful.

So, I started learning how to grow in my listening ability. Listening is a skill. It is a critical skill for leaders.

Most People Don't Feel Heard

People want to be heard but don't feel heard. A classic signal that this is happening is when someone keeps repeating themselves. Or when they start to assert themselves at in appropriate times or contexts. Or when they shut down altogether and stop even trying to communicate.

When there is tension, the best leaders listen. Their first instinct (natural or learned) is to try to understand where other people are coming from. They are also aware that by listening they are valuing those being listened to.

This, on its own, goes a long way to helping people through a tense conversation.

It is only by listening that you can start to identify someone else's interests. It is often by listening well that we communicate value and respect to others. It is simple but not easy.

Not Everyone Knows What They Are Trying to Say

It is not uncommon for a leader to be someone who is more experienced and comfortable knowing what they want to say and saying it. This may not be true for everyone on your team. In fact, many people aren't strongly aware of what they are feeling or thinking. This often manifests itself in stream of consciousness rambling, storytelling without making a clear point, stubborn silence, or heavy use of clichés or stock explanations.

It requires patience and the regular cultivation of a sense of respect, openness, and humility to be able to listen, to ask good questions which encourage more insightful answers and to be able to paraphrase or reframe what is being heard. Often, we need to help people discover what it is they are trying to say.

Not Everyone Is Successful at Saying What They Want to Say

For all kinds of reasons, some people know what they want to say but don't know how to articulate it well or at all. By respectfully helping these people communicate (by patiently listening, by asking good questions, by paraphrasing what was heard to make sure you heard it accurately, by empathizing when appropriate), we can often help these individuals open up and engage. They will often have insights or concerns that are of great value to the group. But even if the value is heavily personalized, being able to engage well helps diminish the tension.

Learning to Listen to a Group

One of the great challenges for leaders is to be able to differentiate what the group wants from what the loudest voices want. It is often not the same. Getting this wrong can leads to ongoing tension.

Because of this, when there is tension, I will often utilize multiple methods of listening. My goal is to gain several angles of perspective. I will most often attempt to utilize at least two or three different methods to gather information or the perspective of the group. Often at least one of those methods includes one which allows for confidentiality or anonymity, such as individual interviews or a survey.

I look for verbal and visual cues that a group is in alignment. I look for where people choose to sit. Do they talk and joke during breaks or does everyone separate or bury themselves in their phones? Is there a willingness to have difficult conversations or does everyone avoid certain issues? Do all individuals seems to engage personally with each other or do some seem to create distance? Does everyone speak up or participate? Does anyone dominate? Are some people physically closing off or pushback from the group?

It's important not to make assumptions that just because a group is quiet, smiling politely and all voting together that they are aligned.

Be exceptionally cautious around self-appointed advocates. They rarely speak objectively.

Resist the temptation to run with the minority voice. This often happens due to a desire for expediency, desire to avoid tension, a lack of curiosity, or agreement with the minority voice. I've sat in numerous meetings where silence is viewed as consensus. In truth, we don't know what it means. So, it needs to be explored.

Ignoring silence might get you through the meeting. If you are using a tool like *Roberts Rules of Order* you might be able to force a vote. You may win people's technical assent. But if you've missed what they really want or think, you might be setting yourself up for significant challenges down the road.

It takes time to listen to a group and try to understand what the general consensus or themes are. It typically takes less time than trying to fix a failing or unsupported initiative. It definitely takes less time than dealing with resistance, mutiny, or sabotage.

Building New Patterns

A close friend of mine recently had knee surgery. Currently, there is a large portion of his knee that is completely numb. The nerves have been damaged. They'll regrow but it will take time. Not forever, but some time.

When it comes to our bodies, most people are aware that they can build their muscles. But they aren't aware that they can also actively and intentionally build their nervous system. In fact, many people have a fixed mindset around things like coordination or balance. In other words, "either you are born with it or you're not."

If you aren't used to balancing on one foot, and you never balance on one foot, your nervous system atrophies to the point where it helps you do just what you are asking it to do, probably just enough balance to stand on two feet and to walk.

When you try to balance on one foot and find yourself being wobbly or even fall over, it is unlikely that you intrinsically can't balance. It's far more likely that you just need to keep practicing. Intentional choices and movements signal to your brain that you are starting to balance on one foot a lot now. That will activate growth of your neural network in your body to the muscles engaged in helping you keep your balance.

Over time, and usually less time than you might imagine, not only will you be able to balance on one foot, but you might be able to jump on it as well.

Teams and organizations are similar. When it comes to tension or conflict, our nervous systems have often taught us to jump into fight or flight mode. We often haven't built the natural tendency to see this as an opportunity, to recognize "We must be on to something important here!" We haven't built the abilities to listen, to stay engaged, to be curious, to be respectful when we feel threatened and so on.

But you can build these. Just like the nervous system can and will grow, you can build out your organization's ability to relate to tension constructively.

The same person who, today, is struggling to stand on one foot, can often learn to jump on one foot. They can go on to learn to dance, or hold yoga poses or do martial arts. They can grow.

The skills required to engage tension will build leaders who are better listeners, make better decisions, less avoidant or reactive, challenging issues can be worked through more quickly, new ideas are no longer viewed as threatening, and the team feels safer to engage, to grow, and to learn.

Your ability, as a leader, to engage conflict builds the capacity in your team.

The growth is slow but can also be steady. You might not see a dramatic change after a few days or weeks of effort. But I can guarantee my clients that they begin to see meaningful change within three to six months and deep change within a year.

It just takes a willingness to see the opportunity for growth that is presented in conflict. It just takes being willing to try and keep trying—you'll get there.

Conflict Builds Leaders and Teams

My hope through this book is to demonstrate and offer tools for you to use the energy and opportunity generated by conflict to build your leadership, the leadership of others, and your team as a whole.

Conflict is unavoidable. It is inevitable. But the quality of it is heavily influenced by you and your choices. The value that can be found, or left undiscovered, is also a choice.

My encouragement to you is to engage with conflict to grow personally, build better relationships, strengthen the structures and systems of your organization and build a resilient and vibrant workplace culture. Conflict makes all of this possible. Embrace it. Let it change you. Help it to change the people and organization you lead.

References

"Conflict | Definition of Conflict in English By Oxford Dictionaries." 2017. *Oxford Dictionaries | English.* https://en.oxforddictionaries.com/definition/conflict

"Founders Online: Thomas Jefferson to Walter Jones, January 2, 1814." 2017. *Founders.Archives.Gov.* https://founders.archives.gov/documents/Jefferson/03-07-02-0052 (accessed October 27, 2017).

Fang, T. 2010. "Asian Management Research Needs More Self-Confidence: Reflection on Hofstede and Beyond." *Asia Pacific Journal of Management* 27, no.1, 155–70. Retrieved from http://doi.org/10.1007/s10490-009-9134-7

Gottman, J.M. 1999. *The Marriage Clinic: A Scientifically Based Marital Therapy.* New York, NY: W.W. Norton & Company.

Kashdan, T.B., and J.E. Roberts. 2004. "Trait and State Curiosity in The Genesis of Intimacy: Differentiation from Related Constructs." *Journal of Social and Clinical Psychology* 23, no. 6, 792–816. doi:10.1521/jscp.23.6.792.54800

McEwen, B.S., and J.H. Morrison. 2017. "The Brain on Stress: Vulnerability and Plasticity of the Prefrontal Cortex Over the Life Course." *Neuron* 79, no. 1, pp. 16–29 (accessed October 30, 2017).

Patton, B., W.L. Ury, and R. Fisher. 2014. *Getting to Yes.* New York, NY: Penguin Books.

Rosenthal, R., and K. Fode. 1963. "The Effect of Experimenter Bias on Performance of the Albino Rat." *Behavioral Science* 8, no. 3, pp. 183–89.

Rosenthal, R., and L. Jacobson. 1963. "Teachers' Expectancies: Determinants of pupils' IQ Gains." *Psychological Reports* 19, no. 1, pp. 115–18.

Sande, K. 2004. *The Peacemaker.* Grand Rapids, MI: Baker Books.

Additional Resources

You can find downloadable copies of the Four Steps to Resolution and other resources designed to help you apply the content of this book at: https://vantageconsulting.org/books/conflictandleadership/

Additionally, you can contact me directly at:

Christian Muntean

LinkedIn   https://linkedin.com/in/christianmuntean
Blog   https://vantageconsulting.org/christianmuntean/
Website   www.vantageconsulting.org

About the Author

Christian Muntean loves working with successful leaders and their teams. His interest in leadership took shape while working in international disaster relief in places like Kosovo, Southern Sudan, and Indonesia. Regardless of how well or poorly a project was funded or designed, success was ultimately determined by the quality of leadership and dynamics of the team.

As a leadership coach and strategy consultant, Christian is recognized for how quickly he helps clients move toward their goals. Clients who work with Christian note his frank, objective approach to solving problems and addressing opportunities. He has become renowned for helping his clients successfully grow or navigate change with practical and easy to implement strategies.

Christian is called on by Fortune 500 companies, governments, and leaders in the entrepreneurial and nonprofit community when they want to develop their personal leadership, help create high-functioning teams, or prepare for growth or change.

Christian has an MA in Organizational Leadership and a BA in Sociology. His wife is a Licensed Clinical Social Worker in private practice and he has three children. As hobbies, he is a strength and conditioning instructor and practices Brazilian Jiu Jitsu.

To reach Christian:
6921 Brayton Drive • Anchorage, AK 99507
Christian@vantageconsulting.org • www.vantageconsulting.org
Phone: 907 522-7200

Index

OTHER TITLES IN THE HUMAN RESOURCE MANAGEMENT AND ORGANIZATIONAL BEHAVIOR COLLECTION

- *Infectious Innovation: Secrets of Transforming Employee Ideas Into Dramatic Revenue Growth* by James Allan
- *21st Century Skills for Non-Profit Managers: A Practical Guide on Leadership and Management* by Don Macdonald and Charles Oham
- *Conflict First Aid: How to Stop Personality Clashes and Disputes from Damaging You or Your Organization* by Nancy Radford
- *How to Manage Your Career: The Power of Mindset in Fostering Success* by Kelly Swingler
- *Deconstructing Management Maxims, Volume I: A Critical Examination of Conventional Business Wisdom* by Kevin Wayne
- *Deconstructing Management Maxims, Volume II: A Critical Examination of Conventional Business Wisdom* by Kevin Wayne
- *The Real Me: Find and Express Your Authentic Self* by Mark Eyre
- *Across the Spectrum: What Color Are You?* by Stephen Elkins-Jarrett
- *The Human Resource Professional's Guide to Change Management: Practical Tools and Techniques to Enact Meaningful and Lasting Organizational Change* by Melanie J. Peacock
- *Tough Calls: How to Move Beyond Indecision and Good Intentions* by Linda D. Henman
- *The 360 Degree CEO: Generating Profits While Leading and Living with Passion and Principles* by Lorraine A. Moore

Announcing the Business Expert Press Digital Library

Concise e-books business students need for classroom and research

This book can also be purchased in an e-book collection by your library as

- a one-time purchase,
- that is owned forever,
- allows for simultaneous readers,
- has no restrictions on printing, and
- can be downloaded as PDFs from within the library community.

Our digital library collections are a great solution to beat the rising cost of textbooks. E-books can be loaded into their course management systems or onto students' e-book readers.
The **Business Expert Press** digital libraries are very affordable, with no obligation to buy in future years. For more information, please visit **www.businessexpertpress.com/librarians**. To set up a trial in the United States, please email **sales@businessexpertpress.com**.

CPSIA information can be obtained
at www.ICGtesting.com
Printed in the USA
BVHW042025050222
628082BV00009BA/879